Drugs and Young People in Scotland

An Introduction for Teachers and others
concerned with Young People

1988: 4th Edition. ISBN 0 906323 23 1

CONTENTS:

PREFACE

Those who work with or in other ways have responsibility for young people often want to be sufficiently well informed about drugs to answer questions and to counsel those who are concerned about drug taking. Part I of this booklet draws together some of the facts about drug use which seem particularly relevant to Scotland. Part II consists of contributions from professional and voluntary groups involved with young people and drug taking. It is hoped that this latter section will not just provide possible pointers for action, but will also help interprofessional understanding and co-operation. It does not attempt to offer prescriptive answers, but tries to show how people in different fields can apply their own skills and experience to drug related problems which they may encounter.

DRUGS AND YOUNG PEOPLE

The word 'drug' is probably derived from the Dutch word 'droog' which means dry. It was applied to the dried herbs, collected for medicinal purposes from many of the far flung parts of the old Dutch empire. Drugs of one kind or another have probably always been with us, as people through the ages used one substance after another in their efforts to cure sickness, relieve pain, obliterate unpleasant experiences or withdraw from the pressures of life. In different parts of the world people have used their own local products and, over periods of what may have been thousands of years, come to recognise the benefits and the dangers of their respective drugs.

Drugs by their very nature carry dangers because seldom does any substance have a single salutary effect on a particular part of the body. On the contrary, while it may be having a beneficial effect on one part of the body, it may at the same time be having a detrimental effect on another part. It is well known, for example, that while aspirin may relieve the pain of a headache it may also be damaging the lining of the stomach. Because virtually all drugs carry health risks they all have some form of control placed upon their use. Some may be bought only in pharmacies; some must be prescribed by doctors; most are readily available only in limited quantities and some may be packed in containers which cannot be easily opened by children. Even substances like tobacco and alcoholic drinks have fairly tight controls applied to their sale in this country.

At the present time in Scotland there is still public concern about the spread of illicit drug use. In successive surveys carried out on behalf of the Scottish Health Education Group since October 1985, this concern is clearly expressed. In each survey people are asked to choose from a list of issues which they think are serious problems in Scotland today. Most mention was made of unemployment, but that was followed by drug misuse. (1)

TABLE 1: SERIOUS PROBLEMS IN SCOTLAND TODAY
Base: All Adults

	1985	1986		1987
	October	April	October	April
Number of People	851	864	905	873
	%	%	%	%
Housing	62	59	68	71
Pollution	28	31	33	31
Unemployment	92	90	90	95
Drug Abuse	91	90	87	86
Road Traffic Accidents	37	31	37	35
Drinking Alcohol	63	61	66	66
Crime	71	74	68	74
Smoking	53	56	58	55
Violence	68	68	67	68
Industrial Strikes	19	20	17	21
Heart Disease	74	67	72	74
Football Hooliganism	53	51	49	43
Aids	28	63	67	75
Glue Sniffing	79	75	72	66
None of These	0	0	1	0
Don't Know	0	0	0	0

Heroin is the substance which causes greatest worry but already there are indications that ruthless traders will push a variety of other drugs. Despite very strict measures to control drug trafficking and the consequent spread of misuse of illegal substances, there will probably always be people who will seek to make money by selling drugs. It must be recognised that what is happening in Scotland is part of complex international changes involving the agriculture and economies of countries in the developing world as well as highly organised crime and a massive increase in international travel and trade. While the availability of drugs varies from area to area and time to time, many potentially harmful substances are available in most parts of Scotland to people of all ages and social and economic groups, both in towns and in the country.

In statistical or population terms the health risks of illegal drugs may be small, but if the problem escalates more and more casualties are bound to appear. Many parents have had anxieties raised by the widespread coverage in the media of the hazards of drug misuse because, apart from the consequences of drug misuse on health and lifestyle, the very fact that they are breaking the law can have a devastating effect on the lives of those even peripherally involved. The complex attractions of drug misuse allied to the determination of those with a financial interest in its promotion mean that the problem is unlikely to go away.

In Scotland there is alarm and anger over the apparent vulnerability of young people to drug misuse. In contrast to the position in the 1960's a larger cross section of society now seems to be involved and the whole scale of the problem is more disturbing. While myths and misconceptions about drugs and the lifestyles of those using them are common, and hard facts are not easily available, few young people seem to doubt their dangers. One problem is that despite their recognition of risks, perhaps even because of it, a large proportion of young people seem willing to experiment.

Among adults, drug misuse by young people arouses a wide range of emotions. Drinking they can understand but resort to heroin and other illicit drugs, even solvents, is seen as strange and subversive. The extent to which drugs are misused will depend on their availability but will also be closely related to the pressures and problems which people face. For those living and working with young people it would be naive to focus attention on the substances alone while ignoring the context which makes the prospect of escape and excitement (for example) so attractive.

This booklet has been prepared on the premise that those working with young people in a variety of contexts already possess a wide range of skills which they can adapt to help young casualties and also to discourage new recruitment to experimentation with illegal and dangerous drugs. Young people are 'street-wise'. They will not be fooled. They know drug misuse takes many forms. They know that people misuse 'over the counter' and 'prescribed' drugs. They know that the use of cannabis is widespread in society and they know that a proportion of the population abuse alcohol. Despite all that, the current problems associated with the increasing use of illegal drugs are different. This booklet seeks to supply facts and destroy the myths that seem to make speaking about drugs so difficult. It also seeks to strengthen the confidence of those working with young people in their ability to adapt their existing skills and expertise to the new problem so that success in tackling drug misuse can be achieved.

PART I

SOME EFFECTS OF PSYCHO-ACTIVE DRUGS

Drugs usually carry adjectives with them. The reason is that the term 'drug' is extremely difficult to define precisely so the substances have to be put in a context of use, eg. 'prescribed' drugs, 'over the counter' drugs, 'illegal' drugs; or their effects have to be described — stimulants, depressants, etc. Psycho-active drugs are those which act on the brain and alter a person's emotions or mental state. Different substances vary greatly in their effects and in their potential dangers, many of which may be increased by 'mixing' drugs and by combining them with alcohol.

Certain effects of psycho-active drugs are worth identifying early on:

Tolerance develops with many drugs when they are used regularly. That is, the body becomes accustomed to the drug and its effect diminishes. As a consequence the user has to take greater doses to regain the original effect. Tolerance may be lost quickly on discontinuation.

Withdrawal symptoms may occur when the regular use of some drugs is reduced or stopped — usually about a few hours after the last use. In some cases the withdrawal symptoms may be extremely unpleasant accompanied by sweating, cramps, nausea, hallucinations, delirium and fits. Withdrawal from heroin is increasingly being described as like a very severe attack of 'flu. Symptoms experienced during the withdrawal period may be due to compensation with other drugs, cigarettes and alcohol.

Drug dependence may have two components — psychological and physical dependence. The former is a strong emotional desire, perhaps even a craving, to continue using a drug or drugs, even if this causes considerable hardship. Psychological dependence may develop in relation to any drug especially if its effects are pleasant or even to other activities such as gambling. Physical dependence occurs when tolerance has developed in the body which displays withdrawal symptoms when deprived of the drug. Some drugs such as barbiturates produce strong physical dependence as does alcohol, with heavy use. On the other hand, certain illegal drugs such as cannabis and LSD produce little if any physical dependence.

While it is easy to conceptualise two different kinds of dependence, in practice they are not so easy to distinguish. They are closely related, especially in those people who are 'poly-drug users', ie. those who use a variety of substances at any one time. Dependence, therefore, may be regarded as a state of sadness, loss or anxiety accompanied by a craving which is experienced when an individual has to give up an activity that is valued or enjoyed.

WHY DO PEOPLE TAKE DRUGS?

There are many explanations for drug use and misuse. Probably the commonest reasons for drug use are curiosity, to begin with, and pleasure thereafter. Many people enjoy the effects of drugs and use them solely for pleasure which is often enhanced by, or combined with, the encouragement of their friends. There is no clear evidence that particular types of personality are especially prone to use drugs. Even so, young people (mainly in their teens and twenties) are especially likely to use illicit drugs and males are more likely than females to do so. Some people use drugs to relieve stress or to solve problems, but most drug use is casual and does not reflect profound stress. Some young people use drugs as a gesture of rebellion. Others simply use them because they are available.

Those who become deeply involved with illicit drugs are often unusual for a number of reasons. In particular, they are commonly young people who whatever their background, have little stake in the workaday world, who live in the most deprived areas or who are estranged from their families. To such individuals the 'drug scene' offers a sense of security and excitement which is often missing in their immediate environment. It is usually to this scene and to the general identity that it confers that young people become dependent. Some do become dependent upon drugs such as heroin, but in many cases the drug itself is not as important to the user as the lifestyle which is associated with the drug.

THE DRUGS PEOPLE TAKE

The list of substances described below does not attempt to be comprehensive, nor are the substances necessarily identified as drugs. 'Solvents' can hardly be described as 'drugs' but may be inhaled for similar reasons, especially by young people. Such substances alter the way the brain works and the user's emotional state. Alcohol and tobacco are also 'mind altering drugs'. These, together with some drugs which are normally available on prescription, are included in this booklet because they may be misused by young people and by older individuals.

DEPRESSANTS

Alcohol

Alcohol is by far the most widely used drug in Scotland. Over ninety per cent of teenagers drink alcoholic beverages, if only occasionally, and alcohol-related road accidents kill far more young people than do illegal drugs. Alcohol is a depressant and sedative hypnotic. It slows down the central nervous system. This is in contrast to the popular belief that alcohol is a stimulant. Drinking alcohol may make people less inhibited and more relaxed but also reduces their ability to perform tasks such as driving.

The effects of alcohol depend upon a variety of factors such as weight, sex and social setting. Females are more affected by a given amount of alcohol than are males. Prolonged heavy drinking can lead to physical dependence, but few young people experience this. The young are far more likely to suffer acute problems, such as accidents, which are due to intoxication. There is no specific 'safe' level of alcohol consumption. People should simply not drink if they are likely to drive. Pregnant women are advised to abstain or to keep their alcohol consumption down to (at most) one or two drinks once or twice a week.(2) 'Low risk' drinking has been identified as up to 21 drinks each week for males and up to 14 drinks per week for females. A 'drink' is equivalent to either a single measure of wine or spirits or half a pint of ordinary beer.(3)

Cannabis (marihuana, marijuana, pot, dope, hashish, bhang, grass, etc)

This is the most commonly used illicit drug in Scotland. Since the 1960's, its use in Scotland has spread considerably. Cannabis is derived from the hemp plant and occurs in two varieties, the hemp type and the drug type. These differ in their potency. Cannabis is usually smoked in a rolled cigarette called a 'joint', but may also be eaten. It is usually smoked along with tobacco.

Cannabis is an intoxicant which produces an effect comparable to that of alcohol. It does not produce strong physical dependence, but some people acquire a strong attachment to the drug and keep using it. The effects users experience are often influenced to a large extent by their mood, surroundings and expectations of the drug. There is also often an important 'ritual' or social element in smoking cannabis. This is frequently a shared experience, with a joint being passed from person to person. Initially like many drugs, it often seems unpleasant or produces no effects. Evidence about the harmful effects of heavy or prolonged cannabis use remains inconclusive.(4) As an intoxicant it certainly impairs the user's abilities to drive or to perform other skilled tasks and in some people causes anxiety and confusion. It is also relevant that the cannabis available nowadays is usually more potent than was the case in the 1960's.

The Opiates — Opium, Morphine, Heroin

These depressant drugs are all derived from the opium poppy. In many parts of the world, opium has long been used both as a medicine and for pleasure. During the late nineteenth century, its use in Britain caused alarm comparable to contemporary concern about glue sniffing or heroin misuse. Morphine, a substance derived from opium, was introduced as a painkiller in the mid-nineteenth century and heroin, an even strong derivative, was produced in 1898. Other similar drugs have been produced, among them Methadone (physeptone) and Diconal (dipipanone). A large number of other pain killers are abused from time to time — these include: Pethidine, DF118 and Dihydrocodene Temgesic Buprenorphine.

In Britain two main types of heroin are used. The first, which is becoming increasingly rare, is medicinal heroin. This is manufactured for medicinal use under the official pharmaceutical name of diamorphine. It is produced as small white pills of 5 mg and 10 mg or as a powder which can be taken by mouth, but it is more commonly dissolved in water and injected subcutaneously (under the skin) or intramuscularly (into a muscle). An initial therapeutic dose would be in the region of 10 mg. When used by addicts diamorphine is usually injected intravenously (into a vein) because this results in more rapid effects. The dose for seasoned users can be many times the initial therapeutic dose.

The second and most common type is illegal heroin, most of which is smuggled into the country. This has been illegally manufactured and is usually available as a powder which is muddy grey, brown or white. Because the conditions of manufacture are not known, nor the extent to which it has been diluted ('cut') with other substances its strength is variable.(5) In this country heroin and other opiates are often taken by 'fixing' (injection) and this in itself adds greatly to the risk of serious illness such as AIDS, liver disease and infections of the blood. Opiates may also be eaten, smoked, snorted or sniffed. Snorting is sometimes called 'chasing the dragon'. It is possible to become dependent upon heroin by using it in this way, although it is less dangerous than injecting it, since it does not carry the risk of AIDS or hepatitis, which is associated with sharing infected 'works' (needles and syringes).

The opiates produce a detached feeling of relaxation, which often has a dream-like quality. With regular use tolerance develops, so that the dose has steadily to be increased to obtain the desired effect. Eventually the heavy user feels unwell unless he or she has regular doses of the drug. In addition to the psychological effects of the drug there is a general slowing down of bodily functions, with constipation, loss of sexual potency and an extreme state of apathy. At this stage the user may find that he or she is deterred from stopping the use of the drug because of the very unpleasant withdrawal symptoms characterised by stomach and muscular cramps, diarrhoea, runny nose and eyes and goose flesh. The withdrawal symptoms vary greatly in severity and are usually related to the duration of use and doses involved. Contrary to popular belief, symptoms of opiate withdrawal may be quite mild.

On the other hand, taking large quantities may cause unconsciousness or even death. Regular heroin injectors have a high mortality rate. Reasons for this include, the presence of impurities in illicit supplies of the drug, the use of unhygienic needles and syringes and the sharing of such equipment. Sharing has long been associated with the spread of various diseases such as hepatitis. Recently the AIDS virus has been spread in this way by drug injectors notably in Edinburgh and Dundee. Death may also occur from overdosing due to the varying strength of illegally obtained drugs or because tolerance has been reduced following a period of abstinence. The unhealthy lifestyle which often accompanies illicit drug misuse reduces resistance to all types of infections.(6,7,8,9)

Barbiturates

Barbiturates are depressants normally (though much less frequently nowadays) prescribed by doctors because of their short-term ability to relieve anxiety and tension. Used inappropriately, beyond their therapeutic dose, they can cause dependence. Large doses, which of course are not prescribed, but rather taken inadvertently or recklessly may induce sleepiness or even unconsciousness followed by prolonged insomnia, confusion and, not uncommonly, epileptiform fits. Mixed with alcohol their effects become unpredictable and frequently dangerous. Like those of alcohol, the effects of barbiturates are incompatible with driving.

Withdrawal from barbiturates may be extremely unpleasant and even dangerous. The drugs are usually taken orally, but if they are injected it is especially dangerous because of their non-soluble additives.

Mandrax

Mandrax (methaqualone) is similar in its effect to opiates, although its chemistry is different. It is easy to become dependent on Mandrax and there is a serious risk of overdose. The latter is particularly marked when this drug is taken in conjunction with alcohol. Mandrax is no longer legally available in the United Kingdom, but supplies continue to come in illegally from elsewhere. It is also present in heroin coming to Europe from Pakistan where it is added to the heroin to make it go further.

Benzodiazepines

These are extremely widely used drugs. The benzodiazepines are the most widely used of the so called 'minor' tranquillisers. The most commonly prescribed are Librium, Valium, Ativan and Tamazapam (chlordiazepoxide hydrochloride) but diazepam, lorazepam, Normison (temazepam) are also now in common use. These drugs undoubtedly serve a useful purpose in reducing anxiety without inducing the marked drowsiness associated with barbiturates, but many people soon develop tolerance and become dependent on them. Prolonged use may lead to depression instead of reducing it. Withdrawal symptoms may follow the sudden cessation of prolonged use. In addition, these drugs have an additive effect when combined with alcohol and many people either accidentally or perhaps even deliberately overdose themselves using such a combination. The use of benzodiazepines is also becoming widespread amongst illicit drug takers.(10,11)

STIMULANTS
Tobacco

Tobacco causes more health damage than do all of the other drugs referred to in this booklet combined. Over 100,000 people in the United Kingdom die each year from tobacco-related diseases and Scotland has the unenviable distinction of having the highest rate of lung cancer mortality in the world. Recent surveys indicate that approximately a third of Scottish teenagers smoke and that girls are more likely than boys to indulge in this very dangerous form of drug use.

Tobacco is a stimulant drug but also has some depressant effects. The short term effects include an increase in heart rate and blood pressure and a fall in skin temperature. Once used to the drug, most smokers are soothed and calmed by tobacco. The main active ingredient, nicotine, is highly addictive and very toxic. Tobacco smoking increases the individual's risk of a wide array of diseases. These include lung cancers, heart disease, stomach ulcers and diseases of the digestive and respiratory system. Even young children who smoke are more likely to have bronchitis and to experience ill health than are those who do not smoke.(12)

The practice of 'snuff dipping' or tobacco chewing is associated with cancers of the gum and cheek (13). Tobacco smoking during pregnancy is associated with reduced birth weight of the babies. Non smokers who have to regularly inhale the fumes generated by smokers run the risk that their own lung functions will be impaired.

Amphetamines

The first large-scale use of drugs by young people in Scotland involved amphetamines ('speed' or 'pep pills', also known as 'sulphate' when in powder-form.) Amphetamine was produced in 1887, but did not become widely prescribed by doctors until the 1930's. Amphetamines were adopted during the 1960's by young people who misused them as recreational drugs. Youthful misuse coincided with awareness of the medical limitations of these drugs. A voluntary curb on the prescription of amphetamines restricted their availability and led to a fall in misuse.

Amphetamines are stimulants. They induce a feeling of euphoria and confidence and suppress appetite. Effects are greatest if injected and this practice is extremely dangerous due to the presence of non-soluble ingredients or impurities in illicit drugs and the risks associated with the sharing of injecting equipment. High doses of amphetamines may produce unpleasant delusions, intense suspicions and disturbed behaviour. Psychological dependence upon these drugs may develop. Although there are no typical physical withdrawal symptoms, withdrawal may cause severe, even suicidal depression. (11.14)

Cocaine

Cocaine is produced from the leaves of the coca plant which grows in South America, South East Asia, the West Indies and Africa. The practice of chewing the leaves of the coca plant has been widespread for centuries in South and Central America. The effects of this are mild in contrast to those of cocaine which may be extremely swift and powerful. Several varieties of the coca plant exist, from only a few of which cocaine may be produced.

Cocaine is a stimulant and is broadly comparable in effect to amphetamines. It is a white crystalline powder. It is normally sniffed but may also be injected. Cocaine generates a strong feeling of euphoria and alertness. It is a matter of debate whether or not physical dependence may be induced, since tolerance does not accompany continued use. Even so, the euphoric effects make psychological dependence relatively easy to develop and withdrawal may be very uncomfortable. For some the effects are so striking and the absence of the drug so depressing that compulsive use of high doses becomes an obsession. Prolonged sniffing may produce tissue damage to the nose. In addition, heavy or long-term cocaine use is associated with physical damage related to many parts of the body. Traditionally, cocaine has been expensive and exotic, available only to those with considerable spending power. Recently there are signs that it is becoming more widely available in the UK. Injecting cocaine, like the injection of any drug, may spread hepatitis and the AIDS virus if equipment is shared. Cocaine may be taken by 'freebasing'. This, like 'chasing the dragon' involves heating the drug and inhaling the fumes. Cocaine misuse is a serious problem in North America. Much of the present concern there relates to a form of cocaine called 'crack'. This is produced by mixing cocaine with commonplace kitchen materials and by heating this mixture. 'Crack' may be smoked and the psychological and physical dangers of 'crack' are much greater than those normally associated with cocaine. In addition freebasing increases the risk of toxic psychosis. (11,15,16)

HALLUCINOGENS (PSYCHEDELICS)
LSD and Other Drugs

These drugs cause concern not because they produce physical dependence, but because their effects are unpredictable. By far the most commonly used of these is LSD (Lysergic acid diethylamide 25) colloquially known as 'acid'. It is possible that native 'magic mushrooms' are currently used as widely as L.S.D. Fungi such as Liberty Cap and Fly Agaric may produce toxic effects, hallucinations, sleep disturbance and nervous tension. PCP or 'Angel Dust' is a cause of wide spread problems in North America. A combination of hallucinogen and stimulant, it is associated with a frightening array of effects. Fortunately it is only rarely used in Scotland.

Hallucinogens alter the way in which the user sees things. They may cause hallucinations and confusion (rather like a delirium experienced by young children with a high temperature). Some users experience changes in their personality after using these drugs and these may be long-lasting. It can be particularly dangerous to body and mind to use hallucinogens while alone, since a panic reaction can be extremely frightening under such circumstances or extremely dangerous exploits attempted eg. 'flying' from a high building. (11, 14)

GLUES AND SOLVENTS
Volatile Hydrocarbons

The Ancient Greeks are reported to have sniffed gases in conjunction with religious rituals. Victorian medical students sniffed nitrous oxide for fun. A large range of solvents derived from petrol and natural gas has become important in our lives because of their importance in aerosols, adhesives and paint preparations. During the past fifteen years, the abuse of glue, solvents, aerosols and related products has caused great public concern. This alarm has been heightened because 'glue sniffing', as it is popularly known, has led to deaths and some of these have involved quite young children. Lurid and sensational media coverage has not helped this situation and may even have led to the spread of this form of drug misuse. There are signs however that the practice is less common than it once was.

Solvents rapidly evaporate at room temperature and, if inhaled, quickly reach the brain and liver through the bloodstream. Their effects are thus felt rapidly. They are depressants and produce intoxication rather like alcohol, although this wears off more quickly. Their smell may linger on the inhaler's breath. Some of these substances are extremely dangerous and deaths have occurred from asphyxiation or heart damage.

While the desired effect or 'buzz' is a happy or euphoric state, this may be followed by confusion, seizures or unconsciousness. It is possible to become dependent on certain solvents with prolonged, heavy use. While all such substances are risky to inhale, solvents, such as dry cleaning agents and aerosols, appear to be more dangerous, being more toxic to the heart, especially if the user gets involved in sudden physical activity. Aerosol sprays are also dangerous since they may cause rapid impairment of breathing due to spasm of the larynx. Use of these sprays has proved fatal. There have been reports of 'sniffing' causing brain damage with, in a small number of cases, permanent impairment of intellectual function and of movement. [17,18,19]. During 1985 and 1986 36 people in Scotland died due to sniffing glues and solvents.

DESIGNER DRUGS

Patterns of illicit drug misuse constantly change and are often localised. During recent years a number of 'new' drugs have gained notoriety, if sometimes only briefly. The range of 'natural' substances such as opium and cannabis has been augmented by illegally produced synthetic 'designer' drugs. Some of these, such as 'Ecstasy' (a hallucinogen) are potent, toxic and are especially worrying since they can be produced with elementary knowledge of chemistry and simple apparatus and ingredients.

THE LAW

For young people the whole lifestyle surrounding drugs misuse may be as attractive as the drugs themselves, if not more so. Also, involvement with illegal drugs presupposes an element of criminal activity. Contact with the underworld and the crime associated with maintaining a drug habit may lead to involvement with the police and serious legal proceedings. It should be recognised that the spread of illegal drugs relies on a whole 'grey economy' dependent on activities such as housebreaking, shoplifting, receiving and resetting stolen goods and prostitution.

British drug control laws apply to many of the substances misused by young people. The principal legislation concerned with the control of drugs in the United Kingdom is the Misuse of Drugs Act 1971 and the various regulations made under it.

Anybody convicted of the unlawful possession, supply or production of drugs controlled under this Act could be imprisoned. Examples of these drugs are as follows:

CLASS A   Heroin, cocaine, morphine, Diconal, Methadone, LSD, Mescalin, opium, PCP, injectable amphetamines.

CLASS B   Certain amphetamines (Methedrine, Benzedrine, Drinamyl, Dexedrin) codeine, cannabis and some barbiturates.

CLASS C   Certain amphetamines (Benzphetanine, Mephentermine and some others, all of which are considered less dangerous or potent), Mandrax and some benzodiazepines (including Valium).

Class A drugs, such as heroin, are regarded as the most dangerous, and offences in connection with these carry the greatest penalties. The Controlled Drugs (Penalties) Act of 1985 increased the maximum penalty for trafficking in Class A drugs to life imprisonment. Class B drugs, including cannabis, are regarded as less dangerous and carry less severe penalties. Even so, such penalties are still appreciable. The maximum penalty for possession of a Class B drug is three months in prison or £1000 fine (level 4), or both on a summary conviction. Even heavier penalties may be imposed on indictment — five years imprisonment or an unlimited fine or both. Anybody convicted of supplying others with a Class B drug such as cannabis could face a fourteen year prison sentence and a fine on indictment. Even the possession of Class C drugs such as Mandrax carries a possible two year prison sentence, plus a fine. Glues and solvents, being very difficult to control, are beyond the provisions of this legislation. Even so, young people in Scotland who are found to misuse such substances may be referred to the Reporter to the Children's Panel, who, if he thinks that the child is in need of compulsory care, will send him to a hearing. Elsewhere in the United Kingdom solvent abuse is not a ground for admission into care. In Scotland there have also been successful prosecutions of persons charged with supplying quantities of solvents to children for the purposes of inhalation in the knowledge that the practice would endanger the health and lives of the children. The Intoxicating Substances (Supply) Act 1985 made it an offence in England, Wales and Northern Ireland to supply people under the age of eighteen with glues and solvents if the supplier has reasons to believe that they intend to misuse them.

MAXIMUM PENALTIES

Penalties / Type of drug	for possession	for production or trafficking
Class A drugs includes heroin, cocaine, LSD	up to 7 years or an unlimited fine or both	up to life imprisonment or an unlimited fine or both
Class B drugs includes amphetamines, cannabis	up to 5 years or an unlimited fine or both	up to 14 years or an unlimited fine or both
Class C drugs includes Mandrax, mild stimulants and benzodiazepines	up to 2 years or an unlimited fine or both	up to 5 years or an unlimited fine or both

Many drug traffickers make vast profits from their illegal activities. To ensure that drug traffickers who are caught and committed do not do so, the Criminal Justice (Scotland) Act 1987 contains measures for the tracing, freezing and confiscation of their assets. The power to make confiscation orders will be restricted to the High Court, but the Act also incorporates the provision, introduced in the Law Reform (Miscellaneous Provisions) (Scotland) Act 1985, which requires the courts, for persons convicted on indictment of drug trafficking, to impose a fine *in addition* to any custodial sentence, unless it is inappropriate to do so. It is expected that this fine will still be used in less serious cases in which a confiscation order would not be appropriate.

Under the Protection of Children (Tobacco) Act 1986, it is a criminal offence to sell tobacco to persons below the age of sixteen.

POLICE POWERS

The Police have power to stop and search anyone if they have reasonable grounds to suspect that that person is in possession of a controlled drug. These powers of search without warrant also apply to vehicles and vessels.

The Police may seize and retain any evidence of a drug offence. The position in relation to searching premises is different. The Police may, of course, search a building with the permission of the occupants. Otherwise a warrant is required. Police in possession of a search warrant, signed by a Justice of the Peace, or a Sheriff, are authorised to enter premises, if necessary by force. It is an offence to obstruct the Police in their efforts to search for evidence of a drug offence.

Because drug-related crime is often bound up with other forms of criminal activity, all police officers are involved in the fight against drugs. All of the eight Scottish forces have specialist drug units and, towards the end of 1986, a drugs 'wing' comprising 21 officers was added to the Scottish Crime Squad. These officers work in close liaison with force drug squads and Customs and Excise Officers.

During 1986 drug related crimes in Scotland rose to 5,318 against the 1985 total of 5,078. This represents an increase of 4.7%. In Strathclyde drug offences fell by 3.6%, the first decrease for several years, while in Lothian and Borders, drug offences increased by 16.1% in 1986, the rise being almost wholly attributable to the misuse of cannabis.

PREVALENCE

Drug taking does not have widespread approval in society and those who indulge in illegal practices are secretive about what they do. Thus the exact level of illicit drug use is not known and is difficult to assess. Surveys provide a useful guide, but no more than that, since some of the information may be unreliable as people may conceal or perhaps exaggerate their habits. Most surveys have been confined to school students or to those in colleges and universities. Few studies have been carried out in Scotland and some of these were carried out a considerable time ago. They may be useful in considering changes in drug taking patterns over time.

In 1968, before the creation of the present local government regions, 18 out of 31 Scottish Directors of Education reported that small numbers of school pupils and young people in further education colleges had been detected using drugs. This experimentation was largely confined to cannabis, but LSD, methaqualone (Mandrax), glues and barbiturates were also mentioned. The Chaplain and Medical Officer at St. Andrews University found in 1970 that 44 out of 159 (28%) students reported having used illicit drugs, mainly cannabis.

Other surveys of Scottish university students published during 1967 and 1971 concluded that 10-14% had used some form of drug. In 1974, the results were published of a study which had collected information from 1,809 young people in Glasgow. Amongst these individuals, 31.5% had used drugs. Cannabis was the drug most commonly mentioned and heroin the least.

In January 1982, National Opinion Polls interviewed a representative sample of 1,326 people aged 15-21 in 101 constituencies in Britain. The exercise, undertaken for the 'Daily Mail' contained a sample of only 57 people in Scotland. The small size of this particular study group should be borne in mind in interpreting the data in Table 2 (overleaf).

TABLE 2: REGIONAL VARIATIONS IN SELF-REPORTED DRUG USE AMONGST THE 15-21 AGE GROUP IN BRITAIN

Drugs ever used	Scotland	North of England	Midlands East Anglia Wales	South of England excluding London	London
	(N = 57*) %	(N = 447*) %	(N = 338*) %	(N = 330*) %	(N = 153*) %
Cannibis	21	15	16	13	28
Amphetamines	8	4	6	3	10
Glues	2	5	1	2	4
Barbiturates	16	2	4	2	3
LSD	8	3	4	2	3
Heroin	7	**	1	1	1
Cocaine	9	1	1	1	3

* Weighted total
** Less than 0.5%
(Source: N.O.P. Market Research Ltd. 1982)

As Table 2 indicates, the level of cannabis use was higher in Scotland than elsewhere (with the exception of London). In addition, the levels of barbiturates, LSD, heroin and cocaine use reported in Scotland were higher than those reported in England and Wales [20].

A more recent study in the Lothian Region followed up a group of 1,036 young people between 1979 and 1983. When first examined, these individuals were aged 15 and 16. Altogether, 15% of males and 11% of females reported having at some tried one form of drug from curiosity. Cannabis had been used by 7% of both males and females. The levels of drug use are shown in Table 3 (overleaf).

TABLE 3: DRUGS USED BY 15-16 YEAR OLDS IN THE LOTHIAN REGION DURING 1979/80.

Drug *	Males %	Females %	All %
Cannabis	7.4	7.1	7.2
Tranquillisers	5.4	5.1	5.2
Glues and Solvents	5.4	4.0	4.6
Valium	4.5	3.8	4.2
Other drugs	4.3	3.8	4.1
Amphetamines	1.9	3.1	2.5
Barbiturates	1.4	1.3	1.4
LSD	1.2	1.1	1.2
Heroin	1.0	0.4	1.0
Cocaine	1.7	0.4	1.0
Mogadon	1.4	0.5	1.0
Opium	0.8	0.5	0.7
Morphine	0.4	0.2	0.3

* In rank order
(Source: Plant, Peck & Samuel 1985) [22]

During 1983, 92% of the original group of Lothian teenagers were reinterviewed. They were then aged 19 and 20. Altogether 30% reported having used some form of illicit drug, 28% had by that age used cannabis, 6% had used amphetamines and 2% had used cocaine.

The use of glues and solvents amongst this group appeared to have waned. This is consistent with evidence that experimentation with several types of drugs is quite commonplace and that such experimentation is mainly only transient and casual. The Lothian study, like many others, showed that young people who experiment with illicit drugs are particularly likely to be relatively heavy drinkers and tobacco smokers. [21,22,23]

There are certainly regional variations in illicit drug misuse. A survey conducted in 1986 indicated that only two per cent of a study group of twelve year olds in the Highland Region had used substances such as glues and solvents, tranquillisers and illicit drugs for 'recreational purposes'. [24]

In 1983 the Scottish Home and Health Department funded the Standing Conference on Drug Abuse (SCODA) to undertake a fieldwork study to provide a realistic assessment of the levels and patterns of drug taking in Greater Glasgow.(25) Through the use of various indicators, the study concluded that it was not possible to arrive at any precise estimates of local prevalence or of the total drug misusing population. It did suggest however that there were around 5,000 problem drug takers in Greater Glasgow at the end of 1983. A problem drug taker is defined as any person who experiences social, psychological, physical or legal problems related to intoxication and/or regular excessive consumption and/or dependence as a consequence of using drugs or other chemical substances (excluding alcohol and tobacco). The Scottish Home and Health Department also funded a similar study in Edinburgh which was conducted in 1985. Again, it was not possible to produce precise estimates but the research suggested that at the end of 1984 there was a minimum of 2,000 problem drug takers in Edinburgh of whom at least 75% would be opiate misusers.

ESCALATION

One of the most commonly voiced fears is that juvenile drug experimentation will lead on to dependence upon, or misuse of, the so called 'hard drugs', such as heroin. The 'stepping stone' theory, that one drug leads to another, is based on the fact that many drug addicts report that the first illegal drugs they used were cannabis or amphetamines. Most

young people who use cannabis and other substances do so purely as a casual, social and temporary activity. The majority try drugs only a few times. Some may experiment with several different drugs for a year or two, and most either discontinue their use or reduce it to become occasional users, mainly of cannabis. Even so, 'polydrug use', that is experimentation with several types of drugs including alcohol and tobacco, is commonplace and taking more than one drug at a time can be very dangerous. It is also true that a minority of young drug experimenters do become regular or heavy users and some become drug dependent or suffer harm. Nevertheless, there is no inevitable progression from experimentation to drug dependence.

WHO GETS INTO TROUBLE WITH DRUGS?

Many young Scots are likely to experiment with drugs, the great majority keeping their experimentation brief and suffering little harm thereby. It is emphasised, however, that serious harm is not restricted solely to heavy or regular drug users. Heavy users are much more 'at risk' than the casual experimenters. But, even casual experimenters, if they dabble in substances like LSD and solvents, could bring tragedy upon themselves and their families. This is especially likely if the experimenter is ill-informed of the possible risks which might be well known amongst older or more 'experienced' drug misusers. The minority of drug misusers who become casualties are not a typical cross-section of young people. While they are drawn from all possible backgrounds, most are rather above school age, and come from working class backgrounds. They are often unemployed or are unskilled manual workers. They frequently come from families with a history of heavy drinking and smoking. Occasionally much younger children cause concern by experimenting with 'drugs' — which in this context generally means solvents.

Most of the young people who get into trouble because of their drug misuse are not physically dependent. Some take overdoses, intentional or accidental, some have had LSD trips. Other fall foul of the law or are pressed into seeking help by parents or friends. Most young people only get deeply involved with drug taking by the appeal of their peers and by the general lifestyle of the 'drug scene'. A high proportion of young drug casualties have many other problems, such as homelessness and unemployment and have previously been in trouble with the police. Many young drug misusers are also heavy drinkers and smokers and often use whatever drugs they can get either 'legally', often by conning a general practitioner, or illegally.

DEPENDENCE UPON ILLICIT DRUGS

As noted above, experimentation with drugs is now widespread amongst young people in Scotland. While most of those who use such drugs do so either occasionally or without harm, a minority become deeply involved with the drug scene and become dependent on a drug or drugs. Doctors are required by law to notify to the Chief Medical Officer of the Home Office particulars of anyone whom they consider or reasonably suspect to be addicted to certain specified drugs. Doctors can only notify addicts who consult them. The majority of drug misusers are not notified because they do not seek help from a doctor. Details of persons notified are not revealed to the Police or any other Government agency. Notification permits doctors to check whether an addict has already been notified and if so what drug treatment if any he or she is receiving. This prevents duplication of prescriptions and thus reduces the possibility of prescribed drugs finding their way into a black market. However, currently the overwhelming majority of those misusing heroin, cocaine and other controlled drugs obtain them from sources which import the drugs illegally.

Between 1975 and 1984, the number of addicts in Scotland, who were recorded by the Home Office as receiving controlled drugs in treatment of their addiction on 31 December, rose from 58 to 137. During the course of 1986, 964 addicts in Scotland were notified at some time. Between 1980 and 1986 Scottish notifications rose almost ninefold, while those in the rest of the United Kingdom more than doubled. The majority of notified addicts are young and male though the proportion of females has increased in recent years. In 1985, in the United Kingdom, 70% were under the age of 30 and 71% were male. Some research in Glasgow in 1981 (25) suggested that only 1 in 10 of heroin addicts in the city had been notified to the Home Office and a study in Edinburgh in 1986 indicated that 1 in 6 was the likely figure. Those figures demonstrate how difficult it is to be confident about the number of regular opiate users. Indeed, they would suggest that the number in Scotland could be anywhere between 6,000 and 12,000.

During 1986, 5,325 new narcotic drug addicts in the United Kingdom were notified to the Home Office, a decrease of about 17% from 1985, most of whom were notified as being addicted to heroin alone or with other drugs.

This was the first fall in new notifications after many years of growth. The number of renotifications of former addicts increased by about 17% between 1985 and 1986. Although total notifications in the UK in 1986 fell by some 700 (8%) from the 1985 figure, this was still well above the number in any previous year.

The new figure for new addicts in Scotland during 1986 is 616, a 17% decrease from 1985 (748) which is in line with the UK figure.

In addition, 348 former addicts were re-notified in 1986. The location of these is shown in Table 4.

TABLE 4: NARCOTIC DRUG ADDICTS IN SCOTLAND NOTIFIED TO THE HOME OFFICE IN 1986

Police Force Area	Number	
	New Addicts	Former Addicts
Strathclyde	383	213
Lothian and Borders	100	71
Tayside	91	54
Grampian	24	3
Fife	8	5
Central	7	1
Northern *	1	—
Dumfries and Galloway	2	1
TOTAL	616	348

* Including Highland Region, Western, Orkney and Shetland Isles.
(Source: Home Office 1987) (26)

The fall in notifications in 1986 from 1985 does not necessarily imply a fall in the level of drug misuse in society generally. As stated above, many other young drug misusers contact different helping agencies and Home Office notifications represent only a minority of those who use heroin and cocaine. In Tayside and Grampian there was a substantial increase in new notifications in 1986 compared to 1985, although the Grampian figure is much lower than Strathclyde, Lothian and Borders and Tayside which account for the vast majority of notifications.

WHAT HAPPENS TO DRUG MISUSERS?

Many young people experiment with illicit drugs for a while and then either stop using them or greatly reduce their use. Even amongst those deeply involved with the drug scene or dependent upon drugs, such changes are commonplace. A 10-year follow-up study of heroin users attending London clinics concluded that 38% had stopped using opiates, 38% continued use, though often at a reduced level and 15% had died. This rate of mortality amongst a group of young people is tragic. Even so, it is clear that even amongst regular drug misusers, a substantial level of improvement or recovery may occur.

Many young people use illicit drugs and alcohol extensively. The majority of these cease the former and much reduce the latter by the time they enter their mid-20's or when they marry. (5,6)

HIV INFECTION AND AIDS

Of the infections which are spread among injecting drug misusers who share injecting equipment, the one which is currently causing most concern is infection with the human immunodeficiency virus (HIV).

In infected individuals HIV is found in body fluids, the largest amounts being found in blood, blood serum and semen. The virus is passed from one individual to another through the exchange of these fluids eg when intravenous drug misusers share needles, syringes and other injecting equipment which is contaminated by blood or through unprotected heterosexual or homosexual intercourse. Babies born to infected women are also infected in a high proportion of cases.

After infection a person remains in normal health for 4 or 5 years or even longer. Then the virus renders incompetent part of the body's immune system and the victim suffers a series of severe infectious illnesses which ultimately prove fatal in a large number of cases. This is the Acquired Immune Deficiency Syndrome or AIDS. It is impossible to distinguish a person infected with HIV from a normal person simply on appearance — a blood test is required. Many drug misusers do not understand this and continue to share equipment or have unprotected sexual intercourse with infected individuals because they think infected people look ill.

At the present time there is no cure for AIDS. A person found to be infected with HIV has a substantial risk of dying within the next 4 or 5 years.

The testing of an individual for HIV infection cannot therefore be undertaken lightly. The implications of both a positive and a negative result must be discussed very fully and carefully beforehand and every effort made to ensure that the implications are properly understood.

A positive result calls for a great deal of counselling support while the individual adapts and comes to terms with the fact of infection and the risk of a relatively early death. Many drug misusers increase their drug misuse and their chaotic behaviour as a result of a positive test.

It has not yet proved possible to develop a vaccine which would immunise people against infection with HIV. The only weapon currently available is to educate people not to expose themselves to any risk of infection. This will involve education against drug misuse for youngsters not already involved, against injecting if current misusers cannot stop immediately and against unprotected sexual intercourse. In addition to public information and education on both AIDS and drug misuse and an expansion of advice and counselling services, other measures are under consideration. These are aimed at harm reduction in an attempt to reduce the spread of HIV infection among drug misusers and from them to the general community. Such measures include, easier access to clean needles and syringes to remove any need for drug misusers to share equipment, the issue of condoms and possibly the introduction (in appropriate cases) of substitute prescribing of drugs to be taken orally as a way of reducing the need to inject. Experimental needle exchange schemes have been established in both England and Scotland. These are under evaluation to determine their effect on the injecting and sexual practices of drug misusers. The results of the evaluation when available will be used in the determination of future policy in this context.

FIRST AID AND EMERGENCIES

Most drugs have effects that are potentially dangerous, so drug misusers may need first aid and sometimes emergency treatment. Problems can be very varied since they often are caused by the interaction of several drugs. The main effect may be for the misuser to withdraw into a dazed state. If so, he or she should be made comfortable and warm in a quiet place until the effects wear off. It is best to lie the person down prone (on his or her front) with the head to one side to prevent choking if there is vomiting.

There is always the risk of unconsciousness and if the person becomes unconscious then emergency aid should be sought either from the family doctor or the ambulance service by dialling 999. If he or she stops breathing before help has arrived, then he or she should be given the kiss of life.

Note any evidence of the drugs and substances that the person may have taken as this will help the emergency treatment. Specialist information can be sought by the doctor from the Scottish Poisons Information Bureau.

Some drugs can cause a state of intoxication rather like alcohol. For a person in such a state the main need is to try and prevent him from having accidents and especially to stop him driving a motor vehicle. The effects of alcohol are often increased by certain drugs.

Drugs can also cause excitement, agitation and hallucinations, which may be quite frightening. People in these states need to be calmed down and prevented from doing themselves an injury. The most helpful thing to do is to stay with persons in such a state and talk to them calmly. It is very important to try and find out before consciousness is lost what drugs have been taken. If the person does not calm down quickly then ring for a doctor or ambulance.

FIRST AID AND AIDS

The aim is to help you give first aid to people who need it and, at the same time, protect yourself from infection.

If you see a person needing first aid, then give it — but take care.

If you have any cuts or scratches, cover them with waterproof dressings. Use disposable rubber gloves if you can. Wash blood splashes off your skin at once with hot soapy water. Clean up spilt blood using household bleach, diluted 1 part to 10 parts of water (Do not put bleach on your skin)

PRACTICAL STEPS

Turn unconscious (but breathing) casualties onto their fronts with head turned to the side and pulled back.

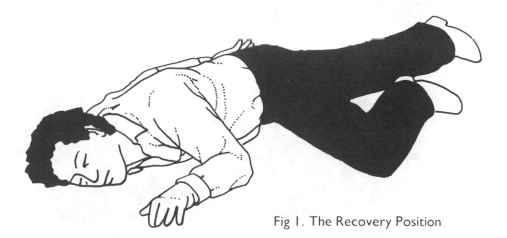

Fig 1. The Recovery Position

In this position they will not choke and airways are kept clear.

Give the 'Kiss of Life' to anyone who is NOT breathing.

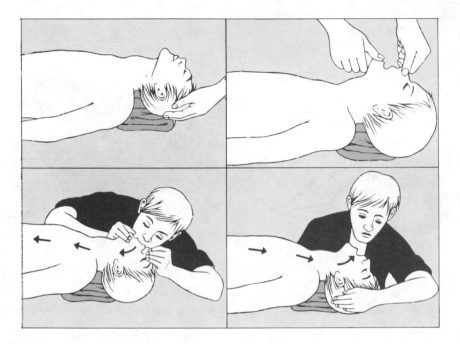

This means—

1. If possible turn the patient on his back.

2. Ensure that there is no obstruction in mouth or throat (e.g. displaced dentures) then bend his head well back and support on folded clothing.

3. Pull his jaw forward.

4. Keep his nostrils closed with your thumb and forefinger.

5. Cover his mouth with yours.

6. Blow until the chest fills.

7. Watch it empty.

8. Repeat the last three actions (5,6,7) each time the chest empties (not more than 20 times in a minute).

Continue until professional help arrives.

There is no evidence that HIV can be passed on through mouth-to-mouth resuscitation.

REFERENCES

Part I

1. Advertising Research Unit (1987) *The Scottish Health Education Group's 1985-88 Tracking Study*. Glasgow: University of Strathclyde.

2. Plant, M.L. (1985) *Women, Drinking and Pregnancy*. London: Tavistock.

3. Royal College of Psychiatrists (1986) *Alcohol: Our Favourite Drug*. London: Tavistock.

4. Advisory Council on the Misuse of Drugs (1982) *Report of the Expert Group on the Effects of Cannabis*. London: Home Office.

5. Stimson, G.V., Oppenheimer, E. (1982) *Heroin Addiction*. London: Tavistock.

6. Thorley, A. (1983) Managing the opiate drug taker. *Medicine in Practice*, 26, August, 666-673.

7. Berridge, V., Edwards, G. (1981) *Opium and the People*. London: Allan Lane.

8. Stimson, G.V. (1973) *Heroin and Behaviour*. Shannon: Irish University Press.

9. Robertson, J.R. (1987) *Heroin, AIDS and Society*. London: Hodder and Stoughton.

10. Curan, V. & Golombok, S. (1985) *Bottling It Up*. London: Faber and Faber.

11. Cox, T.C., Jacobs, M.R., Leblanc, E. & Marshamn, J.A. (1983) *Drugs and Drug Abuse: A Reference Text*. Toronto: Addiction Research Foundation.

12. Royal College of Physicians (1983) *Health or Smoking?*. London: Pitman.

13. Plant, M.A. (1987) *Drugs in Perspective*. London: Hodder and Stoughton.

14. Tyler, A.C. (1986) *Street Drugs*. London: New English Library.

15. Andrews, G., Solomon, D. (Eds.)(1975) *The Coca Leaf and Cocaine Papers*. New York: Harcourt Brace, Jovanovich.

16. Chatlos, C. (1987) *Crack*. New York: Perigree.

17. *Human Toxicology* (1982) 1, 3 June. This volume is devoted to research into glue and solvent misuse.

18. Watson, J.M., Baird, J. & Sourindhrin, I. (1980) Solvent Abuse: The East End Project. *Strathclyde Police Guardian*, 4, 1, 21-25.

19. Scottish Health Education Group (1982) Solvent Abuse: *A report for Professionals Working in Scotland*. Edinburgh: SHEG.

20. N.O.P. Market Research Ltd. (1982) Survey of Drug Use Amongst 15-21 Age Group conducted in January 1982 for the *Daily Mail*. A representative sample of 1326 respondents was interviewed in 101 constituencies. The sample was quota controlled for age, sex and class.

21. Edwards, G. & Busch, C. (Eds.)(1981) *Drug Problems in Britain*. London: Academic Press.

22. Plant, M.A., Peck, D.F. & Samuel, E. (1985) *Alcohol, Drugs and School-Leavers*. London: Tavistock.

23. Plant, M.A., Ritson, E.B. (1976) 'The Scottish drug scene', *Health Bulletin*, 34, 1, 12-15.

24. Bagnall, G. (1987) Alcohol Research Group, University of Edinburgh. Survey of School Pupils in the Highlands, Berkshire and Dyfed (personal communication).

25. Haw, S. (1985) *Drug Problems in Greater Glasgow*. London: SCODA.

26. Home Office (1987) Personal Communication.

PART II
INTRODUCTION

This section brings together contributions from a number of groups involved with potential or actual drug users in Scotland. It is an acknowledgement of the need for a multi-disciplinary response to drug misuse. Often different professional and voluntary groups work in isolation with little knowledge or understanding of the activities and perspectives of other workers in the field. Drugs touch on the day to day work of many professionals and provide an opportunity for collaborative work at a community level. Already in Scotland many groups of workers from the statutory and voluntary sectors have come together to deal with drug related issues. It is hoped that this section will help to promote the sort of understanding which makes these collaborative exercises easier.

The number of similar trends which run through these contributions suggests that despite differing professional perspectives there is a great deal of common ground which can be built on.

1. _Training_. Professional and voluntary workers have a range of skills developed through training and experience. Whether workers realise it or not, these skills are the main resource in tackling the problem of drugs. Training which enables workers to use their existing skills, while at the same time promoting knowledge about drugs and the place they occupy in society, will be a vital part of any anti-drug programme at a local or national level.

2. _Limitations_. Drug taking is a complex phenomenon. Workers can only do so much. The limitations of what can be done are recognised by all the groups represented in this section. But simultaneously there is an acknowledgement of the value of any sort of action which will help to alleviate the situation.

3. _Prevention and Treatment._ To varying degrees, all the groups covered in this part of the booklet will be involved with clients at different stages of involvement with drugs and it is well to remember that drug users do not form a homogeneous group, but rather that they are individuals each with his or her own personality, social background, religion and so on. Some may be young, inexperienced and comparatively naive as far as criminal activities are concerned, whereas at the other end of the spectrum there may be long standing hardened criminals of extremely difficult and intransigent nature. People are different and need different forms of

treatment. However, the same basic understanding of drugs, the circumstances which encourage misuse and the lives of the young people at risk is essential for both prevention and treatment.

4. _Collaboration._ Drugs will touch on all aspects of a community family school, youth club, health centre and social work department. All the contributors recognise the ineffectiveness of tackling the problem within the confines of one particular group and/or institution.

At a community level a number of professionals not formally identified here have a role to play in any collaborative action. For example the police, the clergy, and where appropriate, staff of List D schools, have an essential contribution to make.

As well as offering an insight into the work of other groups, the different sections may prove valuable in their own right. They do not prescribe ways of working or even illustrate the best approaches; merely make suggestions which may prove useful.

Each contribution is a self contained reflection of the work of a particular group. Together they give a flavour of the prevention and rehabilitation work which is developing at a community level in Scotland.

EDUCATION — SCHOOLS

Teachers are well aware that health education courses which emphasise only the risks and penalties associated with any activity are unlikely to influence the behaviour of young people. Similarly, a second approach which only provides young people with 'the facts' as a basis for their health-related decisions, will have limited impact. Modern health education approaches do attempt to give individuals a basic knowledge of health matters as they affect themselves and others. However, such courses also attempt to develop skills which help the individual to make informed choices about health-related matters in their daily lives.

The Schools Council 13-18 Project (1) view on health education was summarised as follows.

'Giving young people a basic health knowledge and understanding of human development.

Helping young people to adapt to change in themselves and their environment.

Helping young people to explore and understand the feelings, attitudes and values of themselves and others.

Helping young people to determine where they have control of their health and where they can by conscious choices determine their future health and lifestyles.'

The project aims to increase the access young people have to relevant health information, but also to help them make realistic decisions by understanding pressures on them to conform to certain patterns of behaviour. Perhaps most important of all the young people get an opportunity to develop and practise important lifeskills which will help them to increase their degree of control of their own lifestyle.

Moving from broad health education to focus on education relating to drugs, it is worth examining the research evidence from evaluation of drug education courses.

1. RESEARCH EVIDENCE RELATING TO DRUG EDUCATION

What conclusions can be reached as a result of the evaluation of drug education programmes in various countries in recent years? The following are some of the main points which can be identified from a review of the literature. (2,3,4,5)

The proportion of educational programmes or courses which have been carefully evaluated is low.

Many have rather vague objectives (for example, they may not differentiate between legal and illegal drugs).

Most resulted in no significant changes in the long-term drug-related behaviour of the target group.

Some increased short-term experimentation with drugs.

Some achieved defined objectives, but there is no clear pattern indicating that some specific methods are likely to be more successful than others.

"Sharon"
age 15

Sharon comes from a middle class family and lives in a pleasant residential area. There is no shortage of money and her parents are concerned for her welfare, but they have been over-protective in the past, and seem more concerned about Sharon's academic prospects, and their own careers. Her guidance teacher is concerned about a deterioration in her school work. Sharon mixes with a crowd older than herself, and is physically mature for her age. She smokes cannabis frequently at parties, and has used alcohol, but she does not really enjoy the latter. She has been offered amphetamine sulphate which she believed was cocaine. Sharon likes to appear sophisticated, and insists that she is able to handle the drug scene. However, she is in fact very afraid of her parents' reaction to her friends and their activities. A Drug Squad raid on a friend's flat has worried her a great deal.

The use of heavy fear messages tended to increase anxiety but did not positively influence behaviour.

Many programmes have clearly illustrated that there is no simple relationship between knowledge gained about drugs, attitudes to drug use and drug-related behaviour.

The complexity of these findings relates to the fact that we are dealing with a problem which far from being a medical issue in a limited sense, has personal, psychological, social and environmental dimensions. We must recognise that an educational intervention will have its limitations and we must be realistic in our expectations about the degree of possible success which will result from education relating to drug use and misuse.

The report by HM Inspector of Schools in Scotland (6) recognised the complex nature of education relating to health issues and also expressed a view on the possible limitations of school health education.

'Schools have not the power of instant effect on behaviour. The mere imparting of specific information about dangers to health does not constitute effective education. Schools cannot be expected to embody, or create, a consensus of health attitudes and behaviour when there is none in society: bad health habits are often symptoms of personal and social problems beyond the reach of schools.'

2. CONTEXT AND APPROACHES

The context of any educational programme relating to drugs is important and may influence the reaction of young people to the programme. In secondary schools drug education may occur in a variety of contexts. It may be part of a health education course which also includes themes such as nutrition, exercise, sex education, safety, etc., or it may arise within the context of science, social education, guidance or religious education. Most schools may include specific topics such as alochol and tobacco and safety in the use of medicines, but not include any overt education relating to illegal drug use. Occasionally, the topic of illegal drugs enters the curriculum in a crisis response to an incident involving illegal drugs which occurs at school.

It is desirable where schools are providing education relating to drug misuse that this should be carefully integrated into the curriculum preferably as part of a social or health education programme. The crisis response or the one-off lecture relates to the feeling that 'something positive must be done' but this response is superficial and may be counterproductive.

There is evidence from early attempts at drug education that young people reject some of the stereotypes which may be portrayed in drug education. The peer group information system is powerful and young people, whether they have experimented with drugs or not, may have considerable knowledge related to drugs and their use. Some courses have tended to portray a stereotype of the 'pusher' as a dangerous stranger who may trick young people into experimenting with drugs. However, in Scotland today reality is rather different as drugs are readily available and the first offer of drugs may come from a friend at school, at the local pub or club or at a party in a friend's house. One piece of research (7) indicated that in a particular situation when young people were offered an illegal drug (mainly cannabis, stimulants and sedatives) on average 50% accepted the offer. Formal health education must therefore take account of people's experience and reflect the real world as people perceive it.

In schools it is sometimes advocated that education which is aimed at influencing the use of drugs by young people should not overtly set out to increase knowledge related to drugs but should give young people personal and social skills which reduce the likelihood that they will become involved in drug use. Such skills include decision-making and self-assertion, and the importance of their development relates to the individual having greater control over his or her own lifestyle. Other skills relating to relaxation and exercise increase the individual's ability to copy with the stresses of modern life. It is difficult to argue with the view that these skills are important. It is however, also difficult to determine the degree to which some of them can be developed within the school curriculum. It has to be acknowledged that people experiment with drugs for a variety of reasons and the use of substances such as solvents, cannabis or heroin may not be simply a measure that people are unable to cope with life. It is too early in the development of courses which include life or coping skills to make extensive claims regarding their success. However, they are increasingly becoming an important part of health and social education courses and early evaluation work is encouraging. (8)

An additional development is the increased degree of active student participation which is involved in health education courses. The use of methods such as discussion groups, case studies, simulation and role play has not yet been proved more effective in drug education courses but it must be stated that there are sound educational reasons for their development. Traditional didactic methods of instruction place the emphasis on the teachers and the learners have a passive role. The participative methods give the learners an active role and an opportunity to use their own language in the organisation of their views. This use of language is central to the learning process and is also an opportunity to rehearse and practise skills which may be important to education about drugs.

The degree to which schools should become involved in overt teaching about drugs will depend on factors such as: the aims and objectives which are considered a priority by the school and the nature and extent of drug use and misuse in the school population. There has been a sensitive debate for some time on the question whether schools, knowing that some of their students sniff solvents, should attempt to minimise harm by giving information to classes on methods of making sniffing 'safer'. This appears to be an issue best dealt with in individual counselling or guidance when a student at risk has been identified. In this way the risk of increasing experimentation amongst those not involved is reduced to a minimum.

In addition to the curricular aspects of education relating to drugs it is important to emphasise the importance of other aspects of school life on factors which can influence the health related behaviour of young people.

The report of the Advisory Council on the Misuse of Drugs (9) referred to this wider role of the school.

'A regard for health education in its widest sense may also be expressed through the whole school environment, the pattern of relationships and routines established, and the self esteem fostered among its pupils. Common in schools, and important, though no one can measure their effect, are the right reassuring words at a particular moment from a respected teacher to a pupil expressing doubt or stress.'

It is impossible to quantify the importance of a positive ethos within the life of the school, but it may be at least as important as the overt curriculum in relation to the personal development of young people. As stated earlier people take drugs for a variety of reasons but one of these is a natural striving for experiences which make the individual feel good, if only for a brief time. It is important that life at school helps to provide a variety of meaningful and pleasant experiences for all pupils. Since some young people may be attracted to drugs because they need excitement and risks in their life, it is important that school provides its share of exciting challenges. One of the important roles of outdoor education centres is to provide a range of new experiences for these young people who may be starved of this type of stimulation.

Similarly all schools have a health promotion function, not merely through their classroom and hidden curriculum of the school. The concept of the 'health promoting school' will be fully explored in the work of the Scottish Health Education Group's joint working party with the Consultative Committe on the Curriculum on Health Education 10 to 14 which is to be published in 1988.

RESOURCES

In 1985 a national planning group was set up in Scotland to develop guidelines on inservice education courses for teachers in Scottish secondary schools. Detailed guidelines for this development were published in Scottish Education Department Circular 1,135 in November 1985. (10)

Derived from the guidelines all Regional Authorities have organised programmes of intensive inservice training courses. The courses highlight the need for Authorities to review their own policies and strategies on drug and health education and senior teachers to clarify their own beliefs and attitudes. Teachers should also explore issues such as the underlying causes of drug misuse, liaison with professional and voluntary groups outwith the school and the particular teaching and counselling skills associated with drug education.

The development of specific resources for drug education has been a feature of health education in the 1980's and certain key resources are mentioned.

As a starting point the book 'Health Education — A Co-ordinators Guide' (Health Education 13-18) (1) provides teachers with a detailed co-ordinators manual which is an invaluable aid for any teachers wishing to develop a general health education programme in their school.

'Drugwise 12-14' (11) is a Scottish drug education programme of lessons for 12-14 year old pupils with trigger video support materials. The materials were developed by a project team in Strathclyde Region in conjunction with The Consultative Committee on the Curriculum. The materials are available from the Scottish Curriculum Development Services (SCDS) and an evaluation report on this development is also available from SCDS (12).

In addition to the Drugwise 12-14 materials the Teachers Advisory Council on Alcohol and Drug Education (TACADE) have produced 'Skills for Adolescence' (13). This includes a student workbook, textbook and a booklet for parents. The materials are only available to teachers who have attended a specific inservice course linked to the materials.

'Drugwise 14-18' (14) is the title of a significant new project developed by a group of UK agencies, including the Scottish Health Education Group. It is a comprehensive course for the 14+ age group in schools and colleges and includes learning materials, a training manual and a curriculum guide. Teachers on the national inservice courses were introduced to these materials and they are being used in a wide range of Scottish secondary schools and colleges.

'Health Education Drugs and the Primary School Child' (15) published by TACADE is designed for 9 to 11 year old children and their parents and introduces drug issues by considering the safety aspects of medicines and household substances.

'Drugs Demystified' (16) published by the Institute for the Study of Drug Dependency (ISDD) is a training course for professionals who wish to increase their knowledge and skills relating to drug education.

'Lifeskills Training Manuals I, II and III' (17) published by Lifeskills Associates are relevant although not specifically concerned with drugs. These attempt to develop important personal and interpersonal skills such as decision making, self assertion and time management.

All the resources listed here place drug education firmly within the context of health and social education and reflect the changing needs of young people. All use participative pupil-centred approaches which seek to encourage young people in the use of information to clarify attitudes and make effective decisions. Approaches like this are challenging and rewarding for the teacher. Support through training and consultation with health education professionals can be obtained from Health Education Departments of Health Boards.

REFERENCES

Education—Schools

1. Schools Council (1984) *Health Education 13-18 Co-ordinators Guide.* Forbes Publications Ltd.

2. De Haes, W., & Schuuman, J. (1975) Result of an evaluation study of three drug education methods. *International Journal of Health Education,* October-December.

3. Dorn, N. & Thompson, A. (1976) Evaluation of drug education in the longer term is not an 'optional extra'. *Community Health.* Vol. 7 No. 3, January.

4. Berberian, R.M. (1976) The effectiveness of drug education programmes: A critical review. *US Health Education monographs,* Vol. 4 No. 4.

5. Schaps, E. (1981) A Review of 127 Drug abuse prevention programme evaluations. *US Journal of drug issues,* Winter.

6. HM Inspectors of Schools, Scottish Education Dept. (1979) *Health Education in primary, secondary and special schools in Scotland.* Edinburgh: HMSO.

7. Dorn, N. and Thompson, A. (1975) *Comparison of 1973 and 1974 levels of mid-teenage experimentation with illegal drugs in some schools in England.* London: ISDD.

8. Botvin, G.J. (1984) The Lifeskills training model in *Health Education and Youth.* Campbell, G. (ed.). Falmer Press.

9. Advisory Council on the Misuse of Drugs (1984) *Report on Prevention.* London: Home Office, HMSO.

10. *Scottish Education Department Circular 1,135* (1985) Edinburgh: SED.

11. Consultative Committee on the Curriculum, Strathclyde Regional Council (1986) *Drugwise 12-14.* Scottish Curriculum Development Service (SCDS), Glasgow: Jordanhill College.

12. Barr I. and Rand J., (1986) *An evaluation report on the CCC/SRC Drug Misuse Package 12-14,* Glasgow SCDS Jordanhill College

13. Teachers Advisory Council on Alcohol and Drug Education (TACADE) (1986) *Skills for Adolescence,* Manchester: TACADE.

14. TACADE, Lifeskills Associates, Institute for Study of Drug Dependency (ISDD), Scottish Health Education Group, Health Education Council (1986) *Drug Wise 14-18* Manchester: TACADE.

15. TACADE, *Health Education, Drugs and the Primary Child*, (1986), Manchester: TACADE.

16. I.S.D.D. (1984) *Drugs Demystified*, London: I.S.D.D.

17. Lifeskills (1985) *Lifeskills Training Manuals I, II and III*. Leeds, Lifeskills Associates.

COMMUNITY EDUCATION

INTRODUCTION

Community education as a profession is well placed to respond to the problem of drug misuse. With its many contacts with different organisations and age groups, the service has the opportunity to become involved in preventive work on a community-wide basis. Its other key role is in providing a front line of advice and help for those experiencing drug-related problems.

With pressure continuing for help from growing numbers of the country's 60,000 volunteer and part-time youth workers, coupled with growing demands from worried parents and community leaders, community education departments and voluntary organisations are responding with action which places the problem within the context of local problems and priorities.

BACKGROUND

Concern among youth and community workers that publicity and information on drug misuse would lead to greater numbers of young people being attracted to the idea of trying drugs, has until recently inhibited any concerted response or lobbying for action by community education departments. The most recent experience has been in the field of solvent abuse, where at first community education workers remained reticent for some time, partly through feelings of inadequacy but partly for fear of being counter-productive, doing more harm than good by raising the issue. In the course of time information among young people increased and the practice spread under other influences and the situation became so open that it became more constructive to discuss the problem than to remain silent. Naturally the weight and emphasis of the problem varied from one locality to another and educational interventions had to be adapted to match them.

In the same way, misuse of illicit drugs seems to have become so widespread that it behoves community education workers to consider their position and to plan their strategies for action in this field just as they have in the past with solvents and alcohol. In all cases of misuse of substances, the issues are complex, depending not only on the particular nature of the drugs but also on the means of supply, the contexts in which they are used, local reaction to those who use the drugs and so on. Perhaps it is because we have generations of experience in the field of alcohol abuse that communities seem less concerned about excessive drinking. But there is no doubt that community concern about heroin and solvent misuse is very real and help needs to be given to the generation of young people who are taking to the new forms of abuse and to the parents who are baffled, disorientated and shattered with feelings of helplessness.

Community education services seem to be caught in a dilemma. They want to tackle the issue and increase everyone's awareness, but are unsure of how to do so in a suitably low-key way to avoid alarm. Finding solutions to this is not easy. However, more recently central Government support for training initiatives has provided a focus for community-based responses. Clear links have been established between the objectives of drug education and the objectives of youth work practice.

APPROACHES/CONCEPTS

Although the settings and informality of approach may differ, the variety of methods outlined in the Education Section is equally appropriate to the work of youth and community groups (eg discussion groups, role plays, introducing new activities and challenges, social education, opportunities for decision making and responsibility). Many of the packs of materials mentioned there may also be of value. A key aspect of informal drug education has been the amount and adaptation of the bewilderingly large number of resources.

These kinds of activities are designed to encourage young people to learn about themselves and what they can make of their lives, in an atmosphere where attitudes are caught and not taught. Generally it is the job of the youth workers to enable young people to recognise that life is a series of choices over which they have control and to assist them in making these choices informed ones. Any discussion about illicit drugs will almost inevitably lead on to consideration of other health topics such as alcohol and smoking. All these topics can only be understood in the light of key issues such as risk-taking, decision making and the development of self-esteem.

However, community education can and should respond not only on the level of individual need. The concerned youth worker, both professional and voluntary, is often uniquely placed to act as a link between young people in need and available help, support and guidance. The local worker can take the initiative in establishing co-operation amongst relevant bodies, and concerned individuals. This allows for the exchange of knowledge and experience, while enabling the development of concerted community responses to the problems faced by young people involved with drugs. A further role for such groups is that of lobbying for commitment and resources from local authorities.

Clearly an effective response must be a consistent response. To this end it is essential for the community education worker to liaise closely with local schools and colleges in order to reinforce their initiatives.

It may be useful, however, to try and identify the variety of actions that could be developed by community education workers as part of a local, concerted plan — a plan that depends on using, supporting and developing the resources of the community.

ACTION

I   *Establishing a local co-ordinating group*

bringing together the local social worker, guidance teacher, health worker, police, community education worker, voluntary youth leader, specialist agency to share knowledge and experience and to develop local co-ordinated support/action.

This has been tried out successfully on other issues where local agencies and interested parties pool resources, information and effort, and is recommended in the Advisory Council on the Misuse of Drugs reports on 'Treatment and Rehabilitation' (1982) and 'Prevention' (1984).

2 *Training*

for local youth leaders, young people and professionals, furnishing them with appropriate information so they know when and how to respond; creating forums for open discussion.

Attitudes need to be changed and myths dispelled. It is better to promote stimuli such as events, activities and projects rather than use scare tactics. Training can introduce leaders to the methods, resources and information which have been developed for drug education.

Youth leaders should be sympathetic to the problems faced by young people and stimulate them to take action. Drug users should not be stigmatised because of their problem.

3 *Promotion of Information*

by involving young people in the research and presentation of information materials locally, to stimulate informed discussion and action, to increase knowledge and help them to make informed decisions.

The information should not only include guidance on where to get help but should include pointers to other exciting and challenging activities.

4 *Developing Support for Local Action Groups*

by providing access to funding and training for parents and community leaders. This will stimulate appropriate action and resources on a self-help basis.

Throughout the country community education is beginning to respond with this kind of action but current provision is piecemeal and reflects individual initiatives mostly in areas of deprivation where the problems are magnified.

CONCLUSION

The community education response hinges on three points:

a) *Priorities*

Drugs may not be an issue for community education in many areas. Forcing the issue onto the agenda is not helpful, but crisis responses to a rapidly worsening situation can be equally ineffective. Local anxiety and activity will determine whether drugs are a priority issue but at this time community education workers should be alert to the drug issue and anticipate difficulties. In addition concerns around drug taking will overlap with and help to influence other growing health issues such as alcohol misuse and AIDS.

b) *Resources*

The resources available within the community are the most effective. Material and information on drugs will be available from Health Board Health Education Departments. Specialist community-based groups may provide appropriate knowledge and expertise. Training is a necessary component of any development of the community education worker's role in this area.

c) *Co-operation*

Bringing together professional, voluntary and parents groups is the only realistic way of tackling the drugs problem in an effective and level-headed way. The success of any action may be limited; drug use is not easy to prevent or control. However, community action which recognises the problems and pressures faced by potential drug misusers may lead to action which will provide young people with legitimate challenges and satisfactions. An improvement of the facilities and services for young people is possibly the best preventative response to drug misuse.

HEALTH SERVICES

At the outset it is worth reiterating some of the basic assumptions which are already contained within this booklet and must be acknowledged in considering any medical response.

1. Any medical response can only be effective when it is part of a broader social perspective.

2. An approach which is 'drug centred' is unlikely to succeed unless it recognises the unique personal, social and economic needs of the individual who presents with the problem.

3. In most cases the doctor will be concerned with multiple drug misuse, rather than physical addiction to any one specific drug.

4. In any individual the susceptibility to treatment may fluctuate over a period of time. Thus while a patient may not respond at one point in time there may be a dramatic change in attitude at a later date. It is important to look for good prognostic signs in individuals and to be sensitive as to when is the best time to become involved deeply with a patient and when to hold back a bit.

5. Strategies based on prevention and early recognition will always be more effective than those which are concerned with rescuing those who have already become severely damaged.

6. Doctors should recognise that their own attitude towards prescribing mind-altering substances is an important part of society's overall view of drug taking.

The majority of drug misusers never come into contact with any medical agency. Amongst those who do encounter medical services, contact may arise as a consequence of the effects of the drugs or of a realtive's concern about the acute or chronic consequences of misuse acknowledged by the patient. Some of these consequences are illustrated in Table 5 (overleaf).

TABLE 5

ACUTE
Acquired Immune Deficiency Syndrome (AIDS)
Overdosage. Poisoning from drug additive
Intoxication
Confusional states (including hallucinations and paranoia)
Septicaemia and other acute infections
Hepatitis
Laryngeal spasm (aerosol sprays)
Epileptiform fits
Conjuctivitis
Nasal congestion
Accidents (falling, choking, burns, etc)

CHRONIC
Physical dependence
Venous thrombosis
Lung and heart disease
Brain damage
Kidney damage
Chronic liver disease
Gangrene
Malnutrition
Ulcerated nasal septum (cocaine only)

Recognising and responding to drug-related problems may be dealt with at a number of different levels as illustrated in Table 6 (overleaf).

TABLE 6: LEVELS OF RECOGNITION OF DRUG-RELATED PROBLEMS

Individual drug misusers
Level 1   Family   Friends
Level 2   GP (Primary Health Care team) Accident & Emergency Dept. General Hospital   Social Work   Police School Counselling Service Voluntary Agencies
Level 3   Specialist Services Community-Based Street Agencies Day care programme Hospital-Based specialist services Detoxification facilities Residential rehabilitation programme

The misuser may recognise the hazards and simply stop, perhaps as a result of advice from a friend or member of the family, or, as a consequence of his or her own increasing experience and maturity.

At the next level two front line non-specialist services are involved. These include, amongst a range of community-based agencies, the general practitioner and the hospital. From time to time these primary level agencies may require the advice of specialist services. Again some of these are medical services, but in other cases specialist opinions may be sought from non-statutory voluntary agencies or from social work. The specialist services are illustrated in level 3. The pattern and extent of these services varies considerably around the country. The medical contribution to this pattern of services is listed below.

GENERAL PRACTITIONERS

The general practitioner will normally be the first point of contact for medical advice and help with drug-related problems. The general practitioner and other members of the primary health care team, are ideally placed to promote education about the hazards of drug misuse. In many cases there will not be any clinical signs to confirm that a drug problem exists and the doctor will have to rely on the story given by the patient and/or relative. Often relatives will describe a history of changes in the supposed misuser's daily habits, behaviour and sleep pattern, with an abandonment of former interests and the acquisition of new acquaintances and marked fluctuation in mood. Unfortunately we all know that such changes are also part of the natural evolution of adolescence and parents should not blame themselves for failing to detect that their offspring have been misusing drugs of suspecting drug misuse when it is not present.

Physical signs may be detected if the patient is under the influence of drugs at the time of the visit — drowsiness, slurred speech, in-coordination, changes in the appearance of the pupils and other eye signs. Further telltale signs may reveal the route of administration. The sores and spots around the mouth and nose of the glue sniffer, or evidence of inflamed and thrombosed veins at injection sites, and abscess of the needle user. The only certain means of detecting that a drug has been taken is by laboratory investigations on the patient's blood or urine. Availability of Laboratory services is uneven and so suspicion of drug misuse may exist for some time before proof is obtained.

If the patient is physically dependent on a drug then he or she may complain of withdrawal symptoms. These are rarely severe, but they may be the principal reason for the patient seeking help and requesting further drugs to maintain the habit and delay the onset of these distressing symptoms.

Assessment in the consulting room is extremely difficult because it relies very heavily on the patient's willingness to be frank about the extent and nature of the problem. Such frankness is rarely forthcoming until the patient and doctor have established mutual trust. This may take a very long time to develop and on first contact a GP will often ask the patient to return at a later time for a more detailed interview and discussion that cannot take place at a routine consultation.

The patient will often believe that the prescription of further drugs will cure his or her problem and policies of substitution have re-inforced this expectation. Drugs are in fact rarely of much value in helping patients whose real need is to make a change in their way of life. Many practices have decided on a 'no substitute' policy. Where this is so it needs to be communicated clearly because the patient may be expecting some substitute. The doctor's main task is often to help assess any physical harm that has arisen, identify social and psychological factors which may underlie the drug taking, and on the basis of this assessment, advise about the risks involved and suggest ways of bringing about a change in this destructive pattern of behaviour. Drug users should be examined for signs of physical illness at an early stage and educated about these. It is very firmly a GP's responsibility to provide a high standard of medical care. In some cases simple advice alone may be sufficient, in others the advice may be supported by information booklets and reference to self-help groups, where such exist. Where the disturbance is more severe or widespread, further counselling and treatment may be necessary. If the general practitioner does not feel equipped to deal with these more complex issues, then he may refer either to social work or to a specialist agency (see below). The GP must consider this action carefully in the light of his or her knowledge of available resources. In some cases the patient has plucked up courage to tell the family doctor and may be disconcerted to find that the response is immediate referral to another agency.

In many situations the general practitioner is one part of a primary health care team which includes nurses and on occasions a social worker. These other members of the team may well take a primary responsibility for providing the support and after-care which the patient and often his or her family will require.

Particular care is needed in advising women who may become or are already pregnant. Most of the drugs mentioned in this booklet are potentially hazardous to the developing foetus and an honest admission of recent drug misuse will help in ensuring proper ante-natal advice and care. It is most important that women avoid smoking, excessive alcohol and drug taking during pregnancy. This is particularly true in the early months of pregnancy and ideally preconception counselling should involve advice about drug taking. The newly delivered baby of a woman who has continued to take heroin up to the time of delivery will need specialist neo-natal care which should be given in a special neo-natal unit.

Withdrawal from drugs may be facilitated by the prescription of transquillisers over a short period of time. Doctors are now very conscious of the hazards of the misuse of tranquillisers and the danger of too liberal prescriptions for these drugs.

Patients who are recognised as drug addicts will be notified to the Home Office and placed on their drug user index. This confidential source may be contacted by doctors as a means of checking whether a user has already been notified and finding out what treatment has already been received. Unfortunately there is good evidence that this register does not at present provide a complete picture of the number of known drug addicts attending medical services. The revised notification form in operation from 1987 asks doctors to indicate if the patient is injecting: it is hoped that this will provide useful epidemiological information about the spread of HIV infection.

Being registered in this way does not imply any right to a particular form of treatment, but it does form a means of reporting that the patient has acknowledged that drug dependence exists. The Scottish Home and Health Department in November 1984 issued guidelines (1) to doctors about the management of patients taking opiate drugs. The guidelines were compiled by a working group of doctors set up by the Department of Health and Social Security as part of the response to the Advisory Council on the Misuse of Drugs Report 'Treatment and Rehabilitation' published in 1982 (2). The guidelines set out good clinical practice for doctors in general practice, psychiatric hospitals, in Accident and Emergency departments, in general hospitals and in the prison medical service. The role of general practitioners in the medical care of drug misusers is well recognised and is of great importance following the advent of HIV and its spread among drug misusers.

COMMUNITY NURSING SERVICES

All nursing staff working in the Community, e.g. Health Visitors, District Nursing Sisters, Community Midwives, Community Psychiatric Nurses, School Nurses, and Nurses working in treatment rooms, are aware of the broader personal social and economic needs of the individual who presents with a problem in the course of their daily work. 'By using existing skills in the assessment of individuals and families, community nurses may be the first to recognise drug-related problems, and will be in a position to offer advice, information, education, support, assessment and referral. By liaison with General Practitioners and other professional staff, an appropriate response can be initiated.' (5)

In many areas Community Nursing Staff are part of a Primary Health Care Team and work closely with the General Practitioner to whom referrals would be made.

The referral of a drug misuser may come from an anxious family or friend and therefore the staff must show an awareness of the needs of the family as a whole.

Strategies based on prevention or early recognition are always more effective than those which are concerned with rescuing those who have already become severely damaged.

Counselling skills to a certain level are used in every situation to highlight the dangers of drug misuse, including the risk of HIV infection and AIDS, preventive measures, and various sources of help available to clients and their families.

The first course of action would be to advise clients and their families to contact the General Practitioner. Other sources of help would include self-help groups, booklets, specialist counsellors and for those requiring further help the General Practitioner may refer the patient to a specialist hospital.

The Health Visitor is available to counsel patients before referral to hospital, to give support at the withdrawal stage, and to look for obvious signs of breakdown in the future. The patient or family may wish referral to the Social Work department as usually drug misuse is only one of the problems encountered.

As discussed above particular care is needed in advising women who may become, or are actually pregnant. It is important to explain the effect of drug misuse, smoking and excessive alcohol taken during pregnancy particularly in the early months. Health education in schools is a necessary preventative measure and Health Visitors may find opportunities to help teachers develop programmes.

Health Visitors involved in the care of pre-school children may have anxieties with regard to young children living with adults who are drug misusers. They would normally make a referral to the General Practitioner.

It is important for them to know the structure of the community in which they work and to know of any particular problem areas.

"Patricia" age 23

Patricia is an unmarried mother, with a 6 month old baby boy. Her boyfriend is in prison convicted of possession of cannabis and heroin. Patricia is a bright, intelligent and attractive young woman. The social work department in her home area have become involved because of her inability to cope with the baby. Patricia comes from a caring family background though her parents have lost patience with her. She left school at 16 and wanted to work in the beauty business. She lived away from home when she went to college and became involved with a group of committed drug users. She uses tobacco frequently, and she prefers cannabis to alcohol. After a few years of fairly casual multiple drug misuse, she became dependent upon heroin. Patricia is unable to respond to her baby and collapsed whilst looking after him on her own. She is afraid that she will be unable to cope with withdrawal from heroin and look after the baby, yet she is terrified that he will be taken from her.

GENERAL HOSPITAL SERVICES

The general hospital most often sees drug misusers as a result of some physical crisis which may or may not be directly related to the drugs themselves. Occasionally some incidental medical emergency brings the patient to hospital and the advent of withdrawal symptoms is the first evidence that a drug problem exists. It is most important that patients, friends and relatives are honest with medical staff about any illicit drugs which have been taken. Suppressing such knowledge may have a very serious affect on the course of treatment.

Emergencies which are more directly related to drug misuse itself are:

1. Overdose either intentional or accidental. Drugs are commonly combined with alcohol in these circumstances.

2. Septicaemic and other serious infections resulting from the use of dirty needles and syringes.

3. Liver disease (Hepatitis) transmitted by syringes and needles (the majority of needle users become carriers of this condition within 2 years).

4. Acquired Immune Deficiency Syndrome (AIDS), which can be transmitted in the same way.

5. Confusion and acute mental disturbance induced by drugs which alter perception, such as LSD, Cannabis and occasionally stimulants such as Cocaine and Amphetamine.

When drug misuse is detected careful assessment is required and this may lead to referral for specialist treatment and rehabilitation.

SPECIALIST SERVICES

The principal hospital-based specialist services offer:

1. Assessment of patients, most often those referred by their general practitioner.

2. General health screening including laboratory testing for the presence of drugs and the detection of hepatitis or other infections.

3. Detoxification (i.e. helping a patient get over withdrawal symptoms) which may involve hospitalisation in severe cases.

4. Rehabilitation which commonly necessitates close liaison and co-ordination with other agencies—this phase may need to continue over a number of years.

Maintenance treatment, substituting the use of one addictive drug over long periods of time, is now used very rarely indeed. It is now recognised that the difficulties in withdrawing from opiate misuse are much less than was formerly thought. If any drug treatment is used, the drug will be prescribed for a short period only — perhaps 7-10 days — and will be prescribed on a day by day basis for oral consumption, often under observation.

However, the role of the maintenance treatment of drug misusers is currently being assessed as one possible measure of how reduction of maintenance treatment could lead to a reduction in the frequency of injecting the spread of HIV among drug misusers will be reduced and the progress towards AIDS of those already infected slowed down.

A large number of other treatment approaches have been advocated for drug dependance such as hypnosis, acupuncture and electro-therapy. Although their adherents claim spectacular successes in certain cases, the methods which have been exposed to scientific assessment seem to be of uncertain value.

The long-term outcome of opiate addiction is not necessarily as gloomy as is sometimes supposed. Follow-up studies suggest that 10% are free of drugs after one year, 25% after 5 years and 40% abstinent after 10 years. Sadly during the same time 2-3% of addicts each year will die of drug-related causes (3). This mortality may increase over the next few years due to AIDS (4, 6).

Despite these specialist services, the General Practitioner remains a key figure in the treatment of drug-related problems.

REFERENCES

Health Services

1.   DHSS (1984) Guidelines of Good Clinical Practice in the Treatment of Drug Abuse.

2.   Advisory Council on the Misuse of Drugs (1982) Treatment and Rehabilitation. London: HMSO.

3.   Thorley, M. (1981) Longitudinal studies in drug dependence. Edwards, G., Busch, C (eds) Drug Problems: Britain; a review of ten years. London Academic Press.

4.   Robertson, J.R., Bucknall, A.B.U., Welsby, P.D. et al. Epidemic of AIDS related virus (HIVLLL/LAV) Infection Among Intravenous Drug Abusers. Br. Med. J. 292, 527, 1986.

5.   Dobson, M. (1984) Responding to Problem Drug Users. Nursing Times No. 21 p 57-58.

6.   Report of the Scottish Committee on HIV infection and Intravenous Drug Misuse, 1986, SHHD.

SOCIAL WORK DEPARTMENTS

Social Work Departments in Scotland have come under increasing pressure in recent years to work with young drug takers. This stems from the growing incidence of drug misuse and the lack of specialist agencies in many areas of Scotland working directly with young drug takers. Those most likely to see an increase in this work are offender specialists, residential workers, prison social workers and those working in a hospital setting. There is, however, evidence that field social workers are also meeting an increase in this problem, particularly in the large housing estates of the central belt.

Social workers are aware of the growing incidence of both prescribed and illicit drug taking. Public concern is mostly over heroin, cocaine and other 'hard' drugs obtained illicitly. However most young people try more than one type of drug, singly or in combination, some of which may readily be bought over the counter, or obtained through doctors' prescriptions.

Social workers who have to work with drug takers are known to feel anxious, perhaps doubting their skills and capacity as helpers, particularly when working with young people. There are two main reasons for this: first, they see themselves as having inadequate knowledge of the drugs used and their effects and second, some workers fear that young people using drugs may kill themselves. The first problem, lack of knowledge can be dealt with readily.

However, the second main cause of anxiety, the fear that a young person who is misusing drugs may die, cannot be so readily dealt with. Those who take drugs may die, and this has to be acknowledged. Social workers who are generally expected by society to be responsible for the wellbeing of their clients feel themselves particularly at risk when working with drug misusers. With the advent of HIV infection and AIDS, this number will sadly increase, often under traumatic circumstances. Social workers will have to deal with, not only the risk of sudden death from overdose, but also the more prolonged work involved in helping AIDS sufferers and their families through the illness and subsequent death.

When involved in any of this work it is vital that the worker who has been involved with the young person and family is given support, not only to deal with his or her own feelings of grief, but also to handle any public criticism which may arise from the death.

Research into drinking patterns, which is likely to be relevant to drugs also, shows that social workers ask clients personal questions about their finances, relationships and legal affairs as a matter of course but do not generally ask them about their use of intoxicating substances. This omission closes off an area of knowledge which would enlighten methods of prevention and treatment. Social workers should be more willing to discuss substance abuse with young people and their families. When they do so it can benefit the parents who often need a professional outsider to help them face the drug taking of a young person in their household.

Assessment is one of the most important skills of a social worker. It is important for social workers to seek information about the use of drugs at an early time in assessment. There are few differences between assessing a drug taker and someone whose problems do no include drug taking, but it is important that specific questions about the extent of use, cost and its effect on the person's life should be asked. Social workers should not rely on, for example, physical symptoms such as needle marks on a client's arm to indicate drug taking. Specific questioning should be used. It is particularly important when reports are being prepared for children's hearings and the courts to ask these questions, as drug taking by young persons may account for other aspects of behaviour and affect the outcome of the referral.

A first step in gaining confidence to work with drug users is to obtain more knowledge about drugs and the effect that they have. Research undertaken in Strathclyde and Lothian shows that social workers expressed more confidence about working with drug takers after specialist training which included details about drugs and their effects. However social workers do not necessarily have to attend special training courses for this purpose. There are books and leaflets available (as listed in Further Reading) giving information about the different substances which are misused and their immediate and long-term effects. While young people will often have knowledge, which may be useful, of taking particular types of drugs, lengthy discussions with drug-taking clients about the effects of the drugs they take are not recommended. A preoccupation with conversation about drugs and the 'street scene' is not a good focus for work and can be a trap which workers fall into when they feel ignorant about the drug scene in general. Clients often prefer to discuss drugs and the drug scene to avoid facing up to and discussing their real problems which will consequently remain unresolved.

After assessment, appropriate methods of intervention should be agreed. In some cases, the worker will be in the fortunate position of having a specialist agency in the area offering a service to which the client can be referred, but in many instances social workers themselves will be expected to offer help to drug takers.

It must be stressed at the outset that the crucial factor is the individual's own decision to stop. The social worker should aim to assist him or her to reach that decision and help to sustain it, but his or her role is one of support and guidance. There may well be periods of abstinence, long or short, before a final decision to remain drug-free is made, and these periods can helpfully be used to consider what external pressures there may be which influence the person's decision to abstain. The process of becoming drug-free may take a long time, years rather than months, and social workers should set their goals accordingly. Drug taking may be not only a dependence but for most people an enjoyable experience, and it is consequently difficult to find persuasive arguments against continuing. In the meantime, it is important to try and help reduce the harm which the young person may incur, and this should certainly be the immediate goal for any worker.

"Michael"
age 14

Michael's problems came to light when he was seen to be acting very strangely at the local youth club where he is an irregular attender. He comes from a large, hard-working, working-class family. His mother died from cancer a year ago. His father is attempting to keep the family together, but he abuses alcohol himself. Michael sees his older brothers drinking heavily and has been drunk once or twice. He uses tobacco, though not at home. He was introduced to cannabis by school friends, and used it in order to be one of the crowd. He has begun to experiment with various unspecified tablets, amphetamine sulphate, and more recently, LSD.

The knowledge and skills that trained social workers already have provided the basis for working with drug misusers, and many of the methods of work which they already employ can be applied in work with young people who are misusing drugs. It is, however, important to think through the special aspects of situations in which drug taking is a feature, and to be clear how they are to be taken into account in applying a particular method of intervention. Appropriate methods of work are as important when dealing with drug takers as with other clients. The type of intervention may well be determined by their level of involvement with drugs — early experimentation, social use with friends, chronic dependence.

Although drug taking may be the primary problem for the client, there will probably be other aspects of his or her situation that are unsatisfactory. Many drug misusers are experiencing difficulties in their family relationships, and in some of these cases it will be appropriate to offer family therapy and to focus on the capacity of family members to enlarge their understanding of their relationships and to make changes in the way they behave towards each other.

Some young people misusing drugs may be best helped through individual counselling. Social workers can select from a variety of approaches. For example, establishing and working within a contract agreed with the young person will be helpful where a focus on short term, achieveable goals is necessary and the young person is ready to collaborate in a clearly worked out programme.

An opportunity to develop new social skills may be particularly helpful for some young people. This will increase their range of personal resources and help to improve self-confidence and self esteem. It will help them to be able to relate to people outside the drug scene and increase their skills in resisting attempts to pull them further into that scene.

It is important that drug takers begin to find ways of enlarging their range of interests and activities and social work agencies can be helpful in introducing them to new possibilities. Programmes can be made available to some younger drug misusers. In other instances the social worker may be able to introduce the young person to a local group in which he or she has an interest.

Community workers can also be of great help. They may be able to assist a community to obtain resources which improve the leisure facilities in the area. They may also be of direct help, where there are existing facilities, in providing alternative activities for some drug misusers. The community worker also has a role to play in encouraging the community at large to become better informed about drug taking and more actively involved in considering how to act to prevent drug misuse among the young people in the neighbourhood.

FURTHER READING

Social Work Departments

Drug Misuse: A Basic Briefing, available from ISDD 1-4 Hatton Place, Hatton Gardens, London EC1N 8ND.

The Misuse of Drugs Act explained, available from ISDD.

How to Stop: (A Do-It-Yourself Guide to Opiate Withdrawal).

How to Help: (A Practical Guide for the Friends and Relatives of Drug Users), both available from the Blenheim Project, 7 Thorpe Close, London W10.

Hallucinogenic Mushrooms, available from Release, 169 Commercial Street, London E1 6BW.

Trouble with Tranquillisers, available from the Granton Tranquilliser Support Group, 126 Crewe Road North, Edinburgh.

Coming Off Tranquillizers and Sleeping Pills, by Shirley Trickett SRN, Thorson's Publishing Group, Wellingborough, Northamptonshire.

Sniffing Solvents by Eve Merrill (with a contribution by Barrie Liss), available from Pepar Publications, 50 Knightlow Road, Harborne, Birmingham B17 8QB.

The Heroin Users by Tam Stewart, Pandora.

Dealing with Drugs by Annas Dixon, available from BBC Publications.

Coping with a Nightmare by Nicholas Dorn, Jane Ribbens, Nigel South, ISDD Publications.

Women and the Aids Crisis by Diane Richardson, Pandora.
Living with AIDS and HIV by David Miller, MacMillan Education.

VOLUNTARY AGENCIES

INTRODUCTION

The voluntary sector has a long history of providing help and support for substance abusers. Recently there has been a rapid increase in Scotland in the initiatives developed to provide advice, counselling and support, both for drug misusers and for their families.

Voluntary organisations, particularly those relating to homelessness, welfare benefits, mental health and offenders have offered help to drug misusers for some time, and this has not decreased with the opening of more specialist drug services in some parts of Scotland. In many cases the specialist provision is geared towards the drug misuser but in many the agency is as concerned with the misuser's family. (This should not prevent anyone contacting any of the agencies identified).

PROVISION OF SERVICES

It is also difficult, and in some ways inaccurate, to give a global picture of the work of voluntary agencies. Individual groups have a particular philosophy and their way of working is determined by the community they support or the needs of whatever group makes up the bulk of their clients.

The style of assistance generally developed has been to give information, support and advice to drug misusers; to help them and their families approach the problems of their own lives, their dependence, withdrawal, and to create new habits and lifestyles. Advice, counselling and support are also offered on HIV infection, its mode of transmission, the implications of being tested for signs of HIV infection and coming to terms with the fact of being infected.

Many of the new voluntary agencies have been developed because of a need identified by the local community and the services offered are nurtured and sustained by the community. In most of these agencies, advice and support is also sought from existing statutory bodies, for example, social work departments and health services.

The voluntary agencies depend largely for funding on charitable trusts, the Churches, voluntary contributions as well as the local statutory bodies and in some cases, direct funding from the Scottish Office.

TYPES OF SERVICES PROVIDED

1. *Advisory/Counselling facilities*

   The basis for all the agencies identified below is an advice and counselling service. They often provide this to those who are not yet prepared to commit themselves to a particular form of treatment, and may provide a link to a number of treatments. Many of these specialist and hospital services are described earlier in the medical section.

   Voluntary agencies may well be the first contact with drug misusers and their families make with helping services. The voluntary sector may be seen by drug misusers as 'safer' than the statutory sector, believing that voluntary agencies are less authorative and will wield less power and control over their lives, and will accept their illicit activities more readily. It is important to remember that no problem is considered too small to be helped by these agencies, and often support and reassurance for the parents of young people involved in the drug scene is a major part of their work.

   Most of the agencies rely on volunteers, in some cases working alongside paid workers. All the various groups have, or are having counselling courses and training for their volunteers, where basic counselling skills are taught.

   Many groups offer either telephone counselling services, for use by friends and relatives, as well as misusers themselves; or person-to-person counselling at the office base. Many of these groups also provide an environment where drug misusers can test their motivation to withdraw from drugs, and be helped and supported through that withdrawal process. Support may also be extended in follow-up procedures for drug-free misusers. All the agencies would generally wish to see any misusers drug-free at the point at which they enter the agency. They should not be 'high' on the drug when they seek help.

2. *Information and Education*

   This is seen by many of the voluntary agencies as a very important part of the service that they provide. Very often it takes the form of basic information on the types of drugs available, and the signs and symptoms of drug misuse. It is imperative that some of the organisations are able to provide this service, either by telephone counselling or by face-to-face counselling.

Because of the specialist skills and experience of voluntary drug agencies, many schools and youth centres make use of their expertise in developing preventive programmes. In working with teachers, community education workers and voluntary youth leaders, the agencies have an important role to play in prevention policies, a role which can be further developed through suitable training.

3. *Day Centres*

    There has been an increase in the number of day centres provided by the voluntary agencies, and most of them are linked to the advisory/counselling services. The aim of the day centre is to provide a drug-free environment, where the drug misuser can begin to rediscover the values of life, and possibly learn a new skill, or develop his or her potential. Often it is simply a place where people can talk and find help and support.

4   *Residential Rehabilitation*

    There are certain organisations which offer residential places to drug misusers. These organisations operate a living and working community life as part of withdrawal from drug dependence, and some expect an addict to stay with them for a considerable time. There is limited provision of this kind at present in Scotland, although various projects are being developed. This often means that someone seeking residential rehabilitation may have to go to Tyneside or further south for this type of care. It is apparent that this type of provision would benefit some drug misusers by taking them away from a lifestyle and peer group which encourages drug misuse. Other misusers may find more valuable day-care, within the context of their own community. Both styles of treatment are necessary although the availability of facilities for both across the country as a whole is still rather patchy.

CONCLUSION

While some voluntary drug agencies have been in existence for a number of years many have only recently received the funding which will ensure a long-term presence. Co-operation between voluntary and statutory workers is fairly well established within the field of drug misuse. Voluntary agencies are an integral part of any community-based action. The support and expertise available goes beyond their more traditional role as specialist rehabilitation and counselling centres. In many cases the voluntary sector provides the major support for parents, who because of their anxiety are possibly among the main victims of drug misuse.

"Andy"
age 19

"ANDY" AGE 19

Andy's mother is a member of a Parents' Support Group organised by a local community worker for the parents of young heroin addicts. Andy is the middle son, a quiet, unassuming boy who shows some understanding and sensitivity about the area of social deprivation in which he lives. His parents are loving, but find it hard to cope with their situation. As a young teenager Andy experimented with alcohol, and was soon introduced to cannabis and amphetamine sulphate. He felt that he could handle these drugs, but he began to experiment with heroin. At first he snorted the drug, but began to inject as his habit developed. He is now addicted, and his mother is still supportive, though she is pushed to the limits of her resources, because of Andy's resort to theft in order to finance his habit. His mother is very concerned about the effect of Andy's addiction on his younger brother.

SUGGESTED READING — GENERAL

Advisory Council on the Misuse of Drugs (1982) *Treatment and Rehabilitation*.

Advisory Council on the Misuse of Drugs (1984) *Prevention*. London: Home Office, HMSO.

Dixon, A. (1987) *Dealing with Drugs*. London: BBC Books

Dorn, N. South N (1985) *Helping Drug Users*. London: Gower.

Edwards, G., Busch, C. (eds). *Drug Problems in Britain: A Review of Ten Years*. London: Academic Press.

Gossop, M (1982) *Living with Drugs*. London: Temple Smith

Orford, J. L. (1985) *Excessive Appetites: a psychological view of addictions*. Chichester: John Wiley & Sons.

Parish, P (1982) *Medicines: A Guide for Everybody*. Harmondsworth: Penguin.

Pearson, G. (1987) *The New Heroin Users*. London: Blackwell.

Plant, M.A. (1987) *Drugs in Perspective*. London: Hodder and Stoughton.

Plant, M.A. (ed) (1982) *Drinking and Problem Drinking*. London: Junction.

Plant, M.A. Peck D.F. and Samuel, E. (1985) *Alcohol, Drugs and School Leavers*, London: Tavistock.

Robertson R (1987) *Heroin AIDS & Society*. London: Hodder & Stoughton.

Royal College of Physicians (1983) *Smoking or Health?* London: Pitman Medical.

Royal College of Physicians (1987) *The Medical Consequences of Alcohol Abuse: A Great and Growing Evil*. London: Tavistock.

Stoppard, M (1982) *Quit Smoking*. London: Ariel/BBC.

Thorley, A., Plant, M.A. (1982) *Drug Misuse*. In Mcreadie, R.G. (ed) Rehabilitation in Psychiatric Practice. London: Pitman, 155-178.

Tyler, A (1986) *Street Drugs*. London. W English Library.

Watson, J.M. (1986) *Solvent Abuse: the adolescent epidemic?* London. Croam Helm.

TRAINING RESOURCES

'Working with Drug Users'
A Video Training Package.

'Working with Drug Users' is an audio-visual training package for professionals which is available for purchase or hire from CFL Vision and the Scottish Central Film Library. The package was directed by Colin Still who also directed 'Illusions' a training film on solvent abuse. It was commissioned and funded by DHSS, the Welsh Office, The Scottish Home and Health Department and the National Health Service Training Authority. The package is intended for use in the context of a training course or seminar and consists of a video-cassette containing 12 separate video modules and a set of written materials including notes for trainers and exercises for course participants. The package is aimed primarily at the non-specialist in the health, social work and other professional group whose work brings them in contact with drug misusers and their families; but it may be of considerable value to professionals already involved in widening their appreciation of differing approaches.

Drugs Training Project
Department of Sociology
University of Stirling
Stirling FK9 GLA
Tel: 0786 73171

This project provides training courses for the staff and volunteer workers in centrally funded drug treatment and rehabilitation projects and for other specialist and non-specialist workers with drug misusers and their families. The project also provides advice and support for trainers and for those with management and supervisory responsibilities for staff working with drug misusers.

Alcohol Studies Centre
Paisley College of
Technology
Westerfield Annexe
25 High Calside
Paisley PA2 6BY
Tel: 041 889 3225

Although primarily concerned with training on alcohol related problems, the ASC also offers training and advice on drug related issues.

USEFUL ADDRESSES

Many individuals and agencies can offer help and advice to young drug misusers. Many of these are equally useful to non-drug takers who may have similar difficulties. Most towns have a counselling service, a hospital, a doctor, social worker, health visitor, minister of religion or some other person who can give confidential, sympathetic advice. Some education authorities have designated guidance teachers, and some areas have special drug liaison committees. Find out whether such agencies or people exist in your area. The following organisations are able to provide materials, advice and information about drugs and drugs misuse.

Scottish Drugs Forum

266 Clyde Street, Glasgow G1 4JH
041-221 1175

This organisation is an indepenent charity funded by the Scottish Home and Health Department. It is the national co-ordinating body for people concerned with drug problems in Scotland. It draws its membership from both the statutory and voluntary sector and is primarily concerned with the support of voluntary drug agencies and parent support groups.

Release

1 Elgin Avenue, London W9
01-603 8654.

ISDD

Institute for the Study of Drug Dependence
1-4 Hatton Place, Hatton Gardens,
London WC1N 8ND
01-430 1991/2/3

SCODA

Standing Conference on Drug Abuse
1-4 Hatton Place, Hatton Gardens,
London WC1N 8ND
01-430 2341

TACADE

Third Floor, Furness House, Trafford Road,
Salford M5 2XJ
061-848 0352

DRUG AGENCIES IN SCOTLAND

A comprehensive list of helping agencies in Scotland has not been included in this publication. For those who need some guidance a booklet of addresses is available. Please contact the Health Education Department at your Area Health Board or write to:

Scottish Health Education Group
Woodburn House, Canaan Lane
Edinburgh EH10 4SG

NOTES